EXPLORERS' LONDON

John Wittich

All photography courtesy of John & Andrew Wittich Photographic Collection
except

Pearly Queen, Beefeater, Trafalgar Square and Piccadilly Circus
courtesy of London Tourist Board

Shakespeare's Globe
courtesy of Richard Kalina, Shakespeare's Globe

Stone Lions – Chinatown, "French House", Gardeners Hut,
Eaton Square, Victoria Coach Station, Church of St. Peter
Morning Mist Publications

ISBN 1 874476 47 0

Published by Morning Mist Publications 1995
P.O. Box 108, Reigate, Surrey RH2 9YP
© Morning Mist Publications

Front cover: Philip Allsopp Graphic Design, Tring.
Typesetting, Origination & Printing: Advanced Data Graphics, Edenbridge.

Dedication

On a wet May evening in 1960 I stood on the corner of Trafalgar Square and Cockspur Street, with Ron Philips, waiting for out first customer wanting to go on an Off-Beat Walk around London.

We waited in vain - nobody turned up. But they did and after that first initial hiccup. *"Off-Beat Tours of London"* was born.

We introduced "London to Londoners" and "London to Visitors" who "turned-up, paid-up and enjoyed themselves".

Now I have to say "Thank you Ron".

We started it and there have been many copyists.

You have now retired but I continue to show people "the sights behind the sights" as we did all those years ago.

To you Ron I dedicate this book.

Sincerely
John Wittich
1995

EXPLORERS' LONDON

John Wittich

Morning Mist Publications
1995

Index

How to use this guide

Explorers' London is divided into ten easy to follow walks. Each walk starts from an underground station which is listed at the beginning of each chapter along with the undergound lines serving that station. Buses connecting with the start are also listed. For easy reference the starting points for each walk along with the connecting underground and bus lines are listed on page viii.

Although each chapter describes a complete walk it is easily possible for you to design your own route placing the points of interest in an order of your choice. It is also easily possible to divide or shorten the walks by finishing at underground stations en route. In some chapters specific suggestions are given.

Each walk is complemented by a map, though it is advisable to also take a detailed map of central London. These are readily available from a variety of outlets.

The publisher recommends that you read the entire walk before embarking on it. This will allow you to familiarise yourself with the area first and perhaps plan which sites you would prefer to spend more time at.

Explorers' London can just as easily be used as an armchair guide to plan your days out in London.

Starting Venues

Chapter	Underground Station	Buses
1	**Monument** Circle, District and Northern Lines (with underground connection with the Bank) ***Bank** Central and Docklands Light Railway	15, 21, 22A, 25, 35, 133, 214, 501, 505, 521, D9, D11
2	**Leicester Square** Northern & Piccadilly Lines	24, 29, 176
3	**Tower Hill** Circle & District Lines	15 , 25, 42, 78
4	**Baker Street** Circle, Bakerloo, Jubilee and Metropolitan Lines	2A, 2B, 13, 18, 27, 74, 82, 113, 139, 159, 274
5	**Victoria** Circle, District and Victoria Lines	2, 1A, 2B, 8, 11, 16, 24, 36, 36B, 52, 73, 82, 177EX, 185, 239, 507, 511, C1, C10
6	**Westminster** Circle & District Lines	3, 11, 12, 24, 53, 53, 77A, 88, 109, 159, 177EX, 184, 196, 511
7	**Leicester Square** Northern & Piccadilly Lines	24, 29, 176
8	**Bayswater** Circle & District ***Queensway** Central Line	12, 70, 98
9	**Tottenham Court Road** Northern & Central Lines	7, 8, 10, 14, 14A, 22B, 24, 25, 29, 38, 55, 73, 98, 134, 176
10	**Tower Hill** Circle & District Lines	15 , 25, 42, 78

* Nearby alternative stations

Southwark
Shakespeare's Theatreland

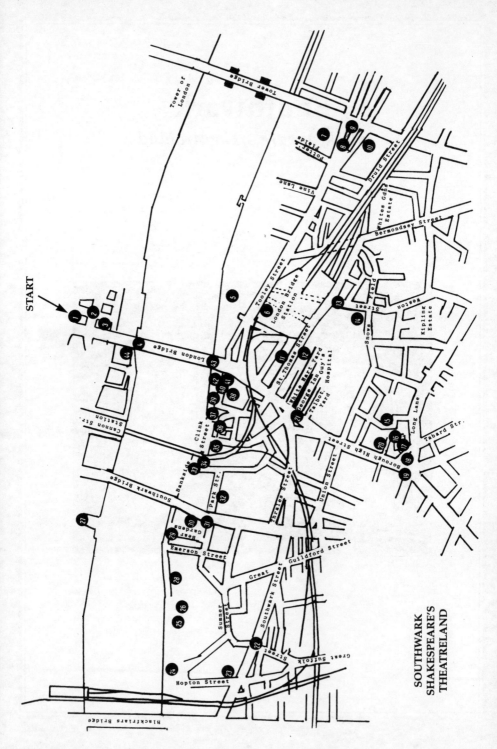

START

SOUTHWARK
SHAKESPEARE'S
THEATRELAND

2

Key to map

1	Monument Underground Station	25	Panorama of the City of London
2	The Monument	26	Bankside Power Station
3	Adelaide House	27	Queenhithe
4	London Bridge	28	Wren's House
5	London Bridge City	29	Ferryman's seat
6	The London Dungeon	30	Shakespeare Globe Museum
7	South London College	31	Site of Rose Theatre
8	Statue Samuel Bourne Bevington	32	Shakespeare and Globe Theatre Memorial Plaque
9	Thomas Guy Plaque	33	The Anchor upon Bankside public house
10	St. Johns Horsleydown Church (site)	34	Clink Prison inscription
11	St. Thomas's Church	35	The Clink Exhibition
12	Guy's Hospital	36	Banqueting House, Winchester Palace
13	Weston Street	37	St. Mary Overie's Dock
14	The Greenwood Theatre	38	Southwark (Anglican) Cathedral
15	Tennis Street		
16	Marshalsea Prison Wall	39	Statue of Roman Soldier
17	Marshalsea Gardens	40	Memorial to London Bridge
18	St. George the Martyr Parish Church	41	The Mudlark Public House
19	Borough High Street	42	Glaziers, Scientific Instrument Makers, and Information Technologist's Livery Hall
20	Angel Place		
21	George Inn Yard	43	London Bridge
22	Southwark Street	44	Fishmongers' Hall
23	Hopton's almshouses		
24	Falcon Point Estate		

Southwark

Shakespeare's Theatreland

**Start: Monument
Underground Station.**

Circle, District & Northern Lines.

**Connecting buses: 15, 21, 22A, 25,
35, 40, 43, 47, 48, 133, 214, 501, 521
D9, D11.**

Time: allow approximately 3 hours.

*T*he development and history of London
can be said to start in three separate
areas. First was the City of London, the
Londinium of Roman times, second was
the Borough of Southwark, the south
ward of the City "over the river". By the
9th century the latter had been created a
Royal Burgh, and had taken on a separate
identity of its own. But first and foremost
Southwark was an ancient town, dating
back to Roman times, and as old as the
City of London itself. It appears
prominently in the changing annals of this
country. All have left their mark on
Southwark. Kings, queens, barons and
Lords of the Realm, holy clerks and lay
celebrities, as well as poets and
dramatists, artists and craftsmen,
scientists and social reformers, all have
been part of the history and development
of this part of London. It is one of the
oldest parliamentary constituencies
returning two Members of Parliament as
early as 1295. It is mentioned in the
Anglo-Saxon Chronicle a compilation of
the history of England parts of which date
back to 892, and may have been either the
work of, or inspired by, King Alfred the
Great, c848-901.

The Chronicle records that in 1016 when
Cnut was attacking the City, he was
repulsed at the bridge and dug a channel
on the Surreyside so by-passing the bridge
and "he entrenched the city so that no one
could get in or go out". It would seem that
Cnut's (Canute), 995-1035, objective was
to control the River Fleet on the west of
the city and so cut off supplies of food and
men to the besieged City. The Domesday
Survey of 1086, records that the bishop
(Odo of Bayeux, and half-brother of the
king – William the Conqueror, 1027-1087,
held Sudwerche with one minster and a
tideway (St. Mary Overie Dock). Early in
the 12th century an Augustinian priory
was founded and continued until the
Dissolution of the Monasteries Acts of the
16th century. It was also in the 16th
century that the theatres arrived in the
area, the first being the Rose (1588). The
Swan followed in 1596, and the most
famous of all the Globe in 1599. With the
theatres came the actors, all parts being
played either by men or boys, and the
dramatists. Here William Shakespeare
became an established actor-playwright-
manager. Born in Stratford-upon-Avon in
1564, he came to London in 1586, at which
time he was probably involved in the
work of The Theatre, or the Curtain
Theatre in Shoreditch. His earliest work
as a dramatist was Henry VI, 1591 all
three parts, followed by other historical
plays, viz. Richard III, 1594, etc. Until the
reign of Edward VI, 1547-1553, Southwark
did not come under the rule of the City of
London, but in 1550, a large portion of the
area was bought from the king and
became the 26th ward of the City. It
became known as Bridge Ward Without,
to distinguish it from Bridge Ward
Within, the latter being London Bridge
itself.

However, the bishop of Winchester who
owned much of the land to the west of the
Minster (now Southwark Cathedral),
retained his ownership of his property.
This is the area shown on maps as "The
Clink" where there was a prison for
offenders against the laws of the Church.
The Lord Mayor of London, Sir Rowland
Hill, formerly took possession on 9th May
1550 when he rode around the prescribe

precinct. John Stow, in his "survey" of 1598 writes "The borough of Southwark which is a ward of London without the walls consisteth of divers streets, ways and winding lanes, all full of buildings inhabited, it hath an alderman, deputies three and a bailiff, constables sixteen, scavengers six, wardmote inquest twenty ". The late 17th century saw a revival of the business in the inns and taverns with the increase of coaching traffic. Many of today's transport services may be seen to have had their origin in the Borough with a twice-a-week service from the Talbot to Guildford, perhaps being a fore-runner of the Green Line Services of later years. In 1750 Westminster Bridge was opened and much of the traffic which had used London Bridge was diverted to the new bridge. When the railways came in the 19th century, the first in London was the Greenwich line from London Bridge. In 1836 some coaching innyards became railway good depots while others disappeared altogether. In 1900 Southwark became one of the twenty-eight Metropolitan Boroughs created by the London Government Act of 1899. Under a major reorganisation of metropolitan local government the Greater London Council was established in 1964 and the London Borough of Southwark was constituted. The new borough consists of the former Boroughs of Southwark, which retained its title, Bermondsey and Camberwell, with a total area of 7,353 acres and a population of one-third of a million.

From being 'a group of houses at the end of the bridge, Southwark has developed into an area of many houses, flats and other tenements'.

Starting Point

(1)   Monument Station.

Opened in October 1868 as Eastcheap, it was renamed Monument in November in the same year. In 1933 a direct, underground, link was built to the nearby Bank Station.

Leave the station by way of the Fish Street Hill exit. Turn right and walk down the hill towards…

(2) The Monument.

Built to the designs of Sir Christopher Wren as a memorial to the Great Fire of London of 1666, in accordance with Rebuilding of the City of London Act of 1667, it stands 202 ft high and is made of Portland Stone. The inscriptions around the base of the column tells of its history and construction. To reach the viewing gallery, near the top of the column, a climb up 345 black marble steps is required, but the view from the top is still one of the best in London.

From the Monument walk up Monument Street to King William Street and the approach to London Bridge.

(3) Adelaide House.

Built between 1921 and 1924, the present building replaces the one which had been the

Head Office for the Pearl Assurance Co. prior to its move to High Holborn in 1931. When this was demolished part of the old London Bridge was discovered, but lack of funds prevented its retention. In the sub-basement of the building there is the former King William Street underground station which was opened in 1890, but closed in 1900 when the Northern Line station was opened. During the two world wars of this century the station was used as a shelter in the event of air raids. It is not open to the public for viewing.

Stay on the same side of the roadway as Adelaide House and walk forward to...

(4) London Bridge.

The present bridge was opened in March 1973 by H M Queen Elizabeth II, having cost five million pounds to build.

Walk to the centre of the bridge and look left towards Tower Bridge, opened in 1894. Looking from left to right can be seen the former Billingsgate Fish Market, the Customs House, built by David Laing, 1774 - 1856, with its row of London Plane trees in front and the Tower of London. Straight ahead is Tower Bridge, with H M S Belfast lying between the two bridges. The last surviving warship from the Second World War, 1939 - 1945, is now open to the public as part of the Imperial War Museum's collection, and gives a "compelling insight into the nature of war at sea". Finally, between the ship and the bridge, there is London Bridge City, part of the redevelopment of the south bankside of the Thames in Southwark, which is well-worth a visit.

Continue to cross the bridge to Tooley Street. Turn left, and, keeping on the left-hand side of the roadway walk along to...

(5) London Bridge City.

When the Upper Pool of London became redundant in the 1960s, the dock facilities having been moved down stream to Tilbury,

the 19th century warehouses were left derelict but have now in the 1980s been developed into London Bridge City with a hospital, restaurants, drinking places and an interesting stretch of the river has been given a new lease of life.

Tooley Street is a strange derivation from St Olave Street, which in turn took its name from the local parish church which had been built here in the 11th century. It was demolished in 1928 when St Olave's House was erected on the site. There is a mosaic of St Olave (Olaf), together with an inscription on the Tooley Street frontage, of the building. The inscription reads:-

"On the ground occupied by this building stood formerly the church of St Olave. This church was founded in the eleventh century in memory of St Olaf or Olave King of Norway who in the year 1014 helped the King Ethelred defend the City of London against the Danes. The original building survived until 1734 and was then rebuilt to the designs of Henry Flitcroft. It was damaged by fire in 1843 and rebuilt afterwards to the same design. It was demolished in 1928. The proceeds of the sale of that portion vested in the Bermondsey Borough Council have been applied to the establishment of a recreation ground in Tanner Street SE1".

Fire has played an important part in the history of Tooley Street during the past three hundred years. In May 1676 over 500 houses were destroyed in a disastrous outbreak of fire, and in 1861 the warehouses along the water front were raised to the ground with a calculated loss of over 2 million pounds. On the latter occasion, the Thames itself was set alight with barrels of burning oil, tallow (wax) and tar. Crowds of Londoners from both sides of the river flocked to the bridge to watch. Charles Dickens, 1812 - 1879, records in "Barnaby Rudge", the Gordon Riots took place here in 1780 - 1781, when the Borough Clink (prison), was destroyed, and not rebuilt afterwards. The Riots, led by Lord George Gordon, 1751 - 1793, marched to the Houses of Parliament to demand the repeal of the Catholic Relief Act 1778. The Act decreed that Roman Catholics were, once again, allowed to take public office, and their worship and schools were tolerated. Later Acts removed all disabilities except that no King or Queen may belong to the Roman Church, and the High Office of Lord Chancellor, Keeper of the Great Seal, are also forbidden to Catholics. Along with members of the Church of England's priesthood, Catholic priests are not allowed to sit as members of the House of Commons, these rulings do not apply to the House of Lords.

On the opposite side of the roadway is.

(6) The London Dungeon.

Founded by Mrs Alexander after her children complained about the lack of a place to visit which was "weird", "creepy" and that showed the more gruesome side of London's history - the torture instruments at the Tower of London were considered tame! Visitors have also given it a label that of being "English eccentricity at its craziest". It is certainly a "must" for those lovers of the grisly and macabre!

Continue to walk along Tooley Street until there is a fork in the roadway.
To the left is…

(7)   South London College.

Before its closure in 1967 this building was the 19th century home of the St Olave and St Saviour's Grammar School, which was a merging of two Elizabethan foundations. It was at the St Saviour's Grammar School that a young John Harvard was a scholar, his family later emigrated to America where he founded Harvard University. A chapel in Southwark Cathedral is dedicated as a memorial to him. There is a purple plaque on the building recording "St Olave Grammar School. 1895 - 1967". Today the building houses a Sixth Form College.

Cross over the roadway where there can be seen two statues.

(8)   Samuel Bourne Bevington, 1832 - 1917.

The first Mayor of Southwark in 1900 to 1902. The sculptor was Sydney Marsh.

Ernest Bevin, 1881 - 1951.

A self-taught politician who, during the Second World War, 1939 - 1945, became Minister of Labour and after, in the Clement Atlee, 1883 - 1967, government was Foreign Secretary. He was the father of the Transport and General Workers' Union, and was affectionately known as the "Docker's K C" from his untiring efforts on their behalf. The sculptor was E Whitney-Smith, 1880 - 1952. It was erected on this site in 1955.

Cross over Fair Street which is in front of the Ernest Bevin bust. Turn left. A few paces up Tower Bridge Road on the corner of Queen Elizabeth Street.

(9)   Thomas Guy Plaque.

"Thomas Guy, 1644/5 - 1724 who built and endowed Guy's Hospital was born at No 7 Pritchard Alley close to this site. "Dare quam accipere". (Rather to give than to receive).

Return to Fair Street. Cross over the roadway, visit…

(10) St John Horsleydown Church (site).

Built on land once owned by Bermondsey Abbey and used as grazing land for their cattle, including horses, hence its suffix. The church was one of the Fifty New Churches Act of 1711 whereby areas of growing population were allowed to restore, and extend their churches, or, where there had been no church, to build a new one. The architect of the church is unknown for certain but some architectural historians claim that it was John James, c1672 - 1746, who produced the designs. He was a Surveyor (architect) to the Commissioners for the Fifty New churches. The church was bombed in the Second World War, and was pulled down in 1947. On the site of the church has been built the offices of the London City Mission. The Mission, founded in 1835, exists for "the spiritual and social uplift of the people of London", and works on the house to house visitation principle as well as evangelism in industry.

Rest in the garden of the Mission, if time and weather permit, and then exit into Druid Street. Pass under the railway bridge, (Crucifix Lane) and into St Thomas Street. Walk along St Thomas Street to...

(11) St Thomas Church.

Near to the site of the church was founded, in 1106, St Thomas's Hospital by the Priory of St Saviour's Southwark (now Southwark Cathedral). The Hospital was, in the 19th century, transferred to Lambeth opposite the Houses of Parliament, but, the rebuilt chapel remained and became a Parish Church. Earlier in this century, at the time of the creation of St Saviour's parish church into Southwark Cathedral, the church became the Chapter House. It served in this capacity until 1988 when a new Chapter House was opened as part of the extensions to the cathedral. There is still, however, in the roof of the building an interesting relic from the past to be seen. Here can be seen in a very sombre setting an operating theatre from the 19th century into which women were led, blindfolded! It was before the days of anaesthetics - to be operated on, watched by fifty or more students. To visit the theatre write to The Secretary Citisights of London, 213 Brooke Road, London E5 8AB (0181 806 4325), visits are normally conducted Mondays, Wednesdays and Fridays between 12.30 and 4pm.

Cross the roadway to...

(12) Guy's Hospital.

The Hospital was "born out of St Thomas's, hospital" and owes its name and foundation to Thomas Guy, 1644/5 - 1724, a prosperous bookseller of Lombard Street in the City of London. His original intention for the foundation was to provide accommodation for sick people who could not be treated in St Thomas's hospital, of which he was a Governor, and those who were incurable and unable to stay in St Thomas's. It was meant to be an extension to the work of the hospital and not to be a rival to it. However, he later decided to separate the two and formed a hospital of some 400 beds. Just as the buildings were ready for occupation he died, aged 80, and was buried in the chapel of the new hospital which took his name. In his will he left to the hospital £200,000, besides other large endowments to charities. In the forecourt of the main entrance to the hospital can be seen Peter Scheemakers', 1691 - 1781, statue of Thomas Guy. It is a 'rare statue' in so far as it is brass, that is bronze without the addition of tin, and is the only outdoor effigy in London so made. In the inner courtyard, through the principle archway there is an alcove from the former London Bridge. When old London Bridge was demolished in the early 19th century several of these alcoves were saved and used as garden ornaments by the purchasers. There is another in Victoria Park in East London, and others can be seen in other parts of the country.

Return to St Thomas Street, turn right and walk along to Weston Street.

(13) Weston Street.

According to Burke's Landed Gentry the area around the street, once owned by Bermondsey Abbey, was acquired by the Weston Family of Woking at the Dissolution of the abbey in 1539. The heiress to the estate, Melior May Weston, who died, unmarried in 1782, left the Maze Estate to her cousin John Webbe Weston. He developed the estate and built Weston Street, and the adjoining streets.

Walk down Weston Street to the junction with Snow Fields where can be seen...

(14) The Greenwood Theatre.

Opened in 1975 by H R H Princess Alexandra, and built by the Governors of Guy's Hospital in memory of Sir James Mantle Greenwood a long-serving Governor of the hospital. Originally a 'live theatre' it is now leased to the BBC who use it as a recording studio for such programmes as "Question Time". It has a seating capacity of 350.

Walk away from the theatre along Snow Fields to Newcomen Street and...

(15) Tennis Street.

Running behind the inns of the Borough High Street's which were once open fields and open spaces for recreational purposes. Here were to be found the tennis courts, a fact hard to believe when walking along the street today. Towards the end of the street the roadway takes a sharp right-angle bend. Here is...

(16) Marshalsea Prison Wall.

Standing opposite the public library is a short stretch of the wall which once formed part of the prison where John Dickens, father of Charles Dickens the Victorian novelist, was imprisoned for debt. Charles would visit his parents here, while he himself had lodgings in nearby Lant Street, and he recorded his impressions of the prison in "Little Dorrit". It is said that the stones of Angel Place are the very ones that were there in Dicken's time.

At the end of Tennis Street is Long Lane. Turn right and walk along to the public open space opposite the church.

(17) Marshalsea Gardens.

On the far side of the gardens can be seen the other side of the wall of the prison. There is an inscription which reads;-

"Here was originally the Marshalsea Prison made famous by the late Charles Dickens in his well known work LITTLE DORRIT".

The gardens themselves were once the churchyard and part of the inner courtyard of the prison. Today it is a quiet spot to take a rest along the way and to admire the Parish Church of St George the Martyr across the roadway.

(18) Parish Church of St George the Martyr.

"In the Vestry slept Little Dorrit" - a touching story from Charles Dickens' story of the same name. She had been locked out from the Marshalsea Prison across the roadway, where her father worked. Her connection with the church had begun when she was baptised there, and it was here later that she married Arthur Clennan, with whom she lived happy ever after! But the history of the church and parish is much older than Little Dorrit and Charles Dickens, having been founded in the 12th century. The medieval church survived until 1736 when it was rebuilt by John Price, at the cost of £9,000. In the old church General Monk, 1608 - 1670, who served in turn Charles I and Oliver Cromwell was married to Ann Radford in February 1653. Pepys in his Diary records his dislike for her, and her intervention in trying to stop his being offered the post of Clerk to the Acts - she failed! It was in the fields around the church that Charles II, 1630 - 1685, was welcomed back to London from his exile on the Continent. The Lord Mayor, Sir Richard Browne, Bt., and the Aldermen of the City of London, together with ALL the inhabitants of Southwark welcomed the king back. In the old churchyard many of the parishioners of the Marshalsea were buried. Among them were Bishop Bonner, Bishop of London in the 16th Century, he died in the prison in 1569, another was John Rushworth who occupied the post of Clerk to Parliament during the time of the Civil War of the 17th century. Like Samuel Pepys he took his notes in Shelton's shorthand and his Collections are

a valuable source of information of the period. The present church stands at the foot of ˎ Borough High Street like a sentry on duty outside a royal palace or castle, with its red brick stone dressings, and the stone tower surmounted by a steeple. Its clock has one dark side - Bermondsey - has given rise to the story that the meaness of the inhabitants of that area in not contributing to the cost has been exploited by almost every historian to date. Inside the church there are many interesting items to look for during a tour. The organ is said to have been in the previous church and to be made up of pipes made, and supplied, by Father Smith, and Renatus Harris, two of the finest organ builders of the 17th century. It was on the organ that the debut of one of the most famous and well loved Christmas hymns was made "While Shepherds watched their flocks by night". It was written by one of the parishioners Nahum Tate, 1652 - 1715, the Poet Laureate of his day. The words are a paraphrase of the telling of the Christmas Story in St Luke's Gospel. He also paraphrased part of psalm 34 in his hymn "Through All the Changing Scenes of Life" for which he collaborated with N Brady, 1659 - 1726. the duo were also responsible for the New Version of the matrical psalms, published in 1696, and dedicated to William III, 1650 - 1702. The ceiling is a reproduction of the 18th century one, and was carried out by Basil Champneys in his restoration of the 19th century. In front of the organ case, in the west gallery, is a Royal Stuart coat of arms which came from the demolished Parish Church of St Michael, Wood Street in the City of London in 1894.

On leaving the church, pause and look to the left where, down the road at the ˎ junction of Borough High Street and Newington Causeway, the stone paving of the road and path finished. It became known as "Stones End" and was the point from which distances to and from Portsmouth were measured. In an Act of Parliament in the 18th century it was mentioned as Blackham Street.

(19) Borough High Street.

Every medieval town or village of any note had a "High Street" and the former Royal Burgh of Southwark is no exception to the rule. The High Street was and still is the most important street of the place. Here trading went on during the daylight hours, here gatherings of the people were called, here processions processed, religious and secular, here all the world and his neighbour met, gossiped or exchanged some profound piece of knowledge. Commencing at the foot of London Bridge and journeying to "Stones End" it was the centre of town - or rather borough.

Walk up the street towards London Bridge, to soon arrive at…

(20) Angel Place

This is the site of the Marshalsea Prison's extension and the one mentioned by Dickens' in "Little Dorrit". The original building was to be found between Newcomen Street and Mermaid Court, but, due to the needs of the day, was greatly enlarged. Founded some time before the reign of Edward III, 1327 - 1377, the site had been used by the Marshall of the King's Household court, hence its name, and was burnt down in 1381 at the time of the Wat Tyler Riots (against the Poll Tax). At first the crimes that were punished here were against the Crown but later extended to include piracy and other crimes committed on the high seas. During the time of religious upheavals, both Catholics and Protestants were held captive here. In later years it became a Debtor's Prison.

Continue to walk up the Borough High Street to…

(21) George Inn Yard.

"When Shakespeare was not imbibing at the Anchor on Bankside he could be found in the George, in Borough High Street", so the story goes. It is London's only galleried inn left from the golden age of coaching. Owned today by the National Trust, it is never-the-less only a shadow of its former self. Three sides of the inn were pulled down in the 19th century with the coming of the railways and their need for depots. The present inn was rebuilt in 1677 after a disastrous fire had destroyed its predecessor. The inn has a number of literary connections John Stow in his "Survay of the Cities of London and Westminster", first published in 1598 refers to it and the other inns of his time. Charles Dickens has Tip Dorrit write a begging letter to Arthur Clenam in "Little Dorrit". Today during the summer months Shakespeare's plays are performed in true 16th century style, using the landing bay of the railway depot as a stage. In the former courtyard picnic tables and benches have been placed for the modern visitors to the inn.

Cross the roadway to...

(22) Southwark Street.

The street was opened to traffic in July 1864, but was not completed for another two years, and cost over half a million pounds to construct. On either side of the roadway today there are warehouses, some of which have been converted into offices, and a multitude of large commercial buildings. "The whole area has become an extension to the City of London", said one local inhabitant. It is certainly not the most inspiring of streets with the 19th and 20th century rubbing shoulders side by side. The eastern end of the street is dominated by the Hop Exchange building in which can be found the Hop Cellar, a wine and chop house owned by the Ball Brothers of London.

Walk along Southwark Street, passing under the railway bridge. On reaching Great Suffolk Street, pause for a moment and look across the roadway where St Paul's Cathedral can be seen on the skyline. Continue to walk until Hopton

Street on the right hand side of the roadway. Cross the road. In Hopton Street can be seen...

(23) Hopton's almshouses.

Founded by Charles Hopton in 1730, for inhabitants of the Parish of Christ Church, Surrey, they were opened in 1752, and thoroughly restored and modernised in the 1980s.

Follow the line of the roadway until on the right Holland Street, formerly Hopton Street. Here bear to the left where can be found...

(24) Falcon Point Estate.

Here the Royal Society of Painters in Watercolours, founded in the 19th century have their Bankside Galleries where both modern and classical artists work is shown.

Hopton Street's roadway ends nearby as a cul-de-sac. Walk ahead until the corner of the Bankside Power Station is on the right. Here is to be found a short flight of brick steps which lead to an earthen mound. Walk to the top of the hillock. Pause and look across the river towards the City of London.

(25) Panorama of the City.

The view from here from left to right includes the spire of St Bride's, Fleet Street, the dome of the Old Bailey with the golden figure of Justice on the top and Faraday House, built in 1932 when there was an uproar over its height (nine stories) obscuring the view of the Cathedral. Behind St Paul's Cathedral can be seen the three tall tower blocks of flats of the Barbican Estate, and a number of spires and steeples of Christopher Wren's churches. These include St Vedast, Foster Lane and the leaden covered steeple of St Nicholas Cole Abbey, shaped like a medieval lighthouse. St Nicholas of Myra is the Patron Saint of lighthouse keepers and of sailors. this is followed by the pinnacled top of the tower of Saint Mary Somerset, and the magnificent steep of St Mary-le-Bow in Cheapside, with the great golden dragon on the top. On the opposite bank of the river, in front of the cathedral, stands the new City of London Boys' School, founded in the 15th century under the terms of the will of John Carpenter, Town Clerk of London. His will provided income to maintain "four boys within the City of London", who were to be called "Carpenter's Children", and to allow them to study at various places of education in the City. Under the terms of the granting of these scholarships the boys were also to sing at the services in the Guildhall Chapel. In 1843 the Corporation of the City of London petitioned Parliament for the setting up of a City of London School and to amalgamate the Carpenter Charity with the new school, thus maintaining an old tradition of the City within the concept of the new school. The new school was opened in 1986.

Walk along the top of the mound until on the right hand side another short flight of brick steps. Descend to the riverside walk.

(26) Bankside Power Station.

Designed by Sire Giles Gilbert Scott, 1880 - 1960, and becoming operational in 1963 the power station was declared redundant in 1980, since which time it has remained unused. There have been several schemes put forward for its future use including turning it into an industrial museum, and even replacing it with a new opera house. It remains a memorial to Scott and to the 20th century industrial revolution. On the left hand side can be seen the now defunct pier that was used to unload materials to the power station.

Continue along the riverside walk and just past the end of the pier. Pause, and once again look across the river to the opposite bank to...

(27) Queenhithe

An inlet in the bankside of the river, it is one of the oldest docks of the City of London. Founded in the time of King ALfred, c 848 - 901, it served the City well until such times as the large ships were no longer able to negotiate their way through London Bridge at which time the Upper Pool, the river up to London Bridge, became the main docking and unloading centre of commerce. In November 1986 the Lord Mayor of London, Sir David Rowe-Ham, unveiled a plaque commemorating the eleven hundredth anniversary of the re-founding of the City by Alfred. To the right of the "hithe" can be seen the tower of St James's Garlickhithe. In the background can be seen the 200m tower of the Nat West Bank dominating the city's skyline. To the right of the tower can be seen the new Lloyds Building, with the blue maintenance cradles clearly showing. The arc is completed by the Southwark Bridge which links this part of Southwark with the City of London.

Continue to walk along the riverside to...

(28) Wren's House.

To the side of which can be seen the modern houses for the Provost and Sacrist of the Anglican Southwark Cathedral with the former's house displaying the coat of arms of the diocese. Wren, 1632 - 1723, came to the lodge in "Wren's House" in the latter part of his life. If he did not want to be disturbed he told the housekeeper to say to any unwanted visitors that he was designing St Paul's and did not want to be interrupted. There is no evidence that Wren owned the house, but only that he was a lodger, the house being part of the nearby iron-foundry, of which a certain Mr Jones was both the manager and a friend of Wren's. The railings for the cathedral were cast at Lamberhurst and were finished in the foundry here. On the site of the foundry there has now been built a replica of the Globe Theatre, and Shakespearian Centre.

Walk on past Emerson Street, to the Bear Gardens.

(29) Ferryman's Seat.

At the river end of the Gardens, set into the wall of a building, is the seat that was used by the ferry-man who spent his life ferrying men and women across the river to the 16th and 17th century theatres that stood here.

Walk down the Bear Gardens.

(30) Shakespeare Globe Museum.

Built on the site of the Bear Gardens where, up to the 17th century, bear baiting was a popular pastime among the citizens of London and Southwark. One of the favourite pastimes of

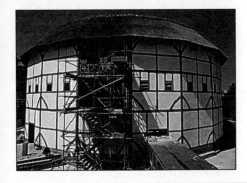

the period was to starve a bear for several days, bring it here, tie it to a stake in the centre of the arena and to set dogs on it. Bets would be placed as to which, if any, dogs would survive the ordeal. Sometimes the bear broke loose from the stake and ravished the dogs and even their handlers. The plaque on the side of the building reads "Historic Southwark. On this site was built the Davies Amphitheatre 1662 - 1682 the last bear-baiting ring of Bankside. Visited by Samuel Pepys and John Evelyn. To the north from mid-16th century was the Bear Garden. A bear-baiting ring, visited by Queen Elizabeth I, had replaced the Hope Playhouse in 1614 - 1656. Built for plays and bear-baiting and where Ben Johnson's, 1572 - 1637, play "Bartholomew Fayre" was first performed (in 1614). The museum is open from 10am to 5pm Tuesdays to Saturdays, and Sunday from 2pm to 5.30pm, and is well worth a visit. There is a fee to be paid.

At the end of the Bear Gardens turn left and walk along Park Street.

(31) Rose Theatre, site of.

On the side of the building there is a street sign which reads "Rose Alley", here, at the end of 1988, excavations took place prior to the building on the site of a new office block. The

theatre was built c 1587 by the playwright Philip Henslow, who before his death in 1616 rebuilt and managed the Rose Theatre, where he subsequently employed a number of minor Elizabethan dramatists. The site was fully excavated in 1989 and revealed the general outline of his theatre. While it was not a large building, its discovery revealed the layout of the theatre, but despite several attempts, the building of a new office building was allowed to go ahead. It is hoped that some form of access to the site will be allowed by the owners of the site, and that the valuable remains will be seen by future generations of students of the theatre and members of the general public.

Continue to walk ahead along Park Street and on the right hand side of the roadway will be seen...

(32) Shakespeare and Globe Memorial plaque.

The inscription reads "Here stood the Globe Playhouse of Shakespeare 1593 - 1613". The lower inscription reads "Commemorated by the Shakespear Reading Society of London and by subscribers in the United Kingdom and India". Behind the head and shoulders of William Shakespeare can be seen the scene of Bankside in the time of the Bard, with London Bridge, complete with houses, and the gate-house at the south end and the heads of those who had been executed in London placed on the top of stakes. The original of 'counting heads' dates from these times when it was the duty of the gate-keeper to count the heads of the executed every morning to ensure that they were all there. It was common practice for friends and relations to steal the heads of their loved ones and give them a decent Christian burial - even if the rest of the bodies had been disposed of in quick lime pits near the site of their execution.

Across the roadway from the plaque are the new offices of the Financial Times, who moved here from their post-war building in Cannon Street in 1988.

From the Shakespearian plaque walk ahead until the "T" junction with Bankside to the left. Turn Left.

(33) The Anchor upon Bankside.

Hidden among the warehouses, half obscured by a railway bridge is the Anchor Public House. The stories that are told of this house are numerous but none of them lack that taste of tales well told. Here came Shakespeare, between acts at the nearby Globe Playhouse, and later here came Doctor Samuel Johnson who obviously found the compilation of the first English Dictionary thirsty work! Or perhaps you will listen to the stories of the river pirates coming into the bar and selling their ill-gotten gains to the barman. There are tales too of the escapees from the nearby Clink Prison across the roadway coming into the inn and never seen leaving. There is a secret hiding place in the centre of the building - pass through a cupboard and find yourself in the safety of a hidden 'hidey-hole'. Here came the Press Gangs of the 17th century whose sole job in life was to impress on the fit and healthy man that he should join the Royal Navy.

A quick, sharp, hit on the head, and several hours later the victim would waken aboard a ship of the Navy. The building was destroyed by fire in 1676 and rebuilt, having been used as a viewing place by the citizens of London during the Great Fire of 1666, when 5/6th of the City of London was destroyed. The house was famous for its Russian Imperial Stout brewed specially for the Empress of Russia. It was a Porter, and consisted of a mixture of ale beer, and twopenny (a pale, small beer of 18th century London, which sold at 4d a quart but was a beer of lesser gravity). It is said that one pint of the Stout and you woke up in the Royal Navy! The inn was a popular place of entertainment in the 18th century being so close to the 'stews' (the red-light area of the time). The new permanent Bankside Terrace where customers can sit and enjoy their eats and drinks is part of the redevelopment of the area - and very good it is too!

From the Bankside Terrace it is a short walk to the plaque recording the imprisonments of 'heretics' of the 16th and 17th century.

(34) Clink Prison Inscription.

The painted board reads "Near this site stood the Clink Prison", and goes on to record some of the protesters of the 17th century who were incarcerated in the prison.

Pass under the railway arch where can be seen two blocked-in archways under which railway lines once ran enabling goods to be loaded and unloaded from the railway trucks that were shunted from Bricklayers Arms depot underneath the railway viaduct above here. On the walls can still be seen the wall-mounted cranes that were used in the loading and unloading operations.

(35) The Clink Exhibition.

A new exhibition, opened in 1989, on the site of the notorious Clink Prison. Here can be witnessed and enjoyed the history of the Clink Prison on its original site. The exhibition is open seven days a week from 10am to 10pm - there is an entrance fee. The prison, which came under the jurisdiction of the Bishops of Winchester was used by them to imprison persons who were alleged to have committed crimes against the Canon (Church) Law as opposed to the Civil Law of the land. The name comes from the French word "Clenche" meaning a catch or bolt attached to the outside of the door thereby making it impossible for somebody inside to escape.

Just past "The Clink Exhibition" is Stoney Street and then can be seen…

(36) Banqueting House of the Palace of the Bishops of Winchester.

Here in the 12th century, the Bishops of Winchester, in whose diocese Southwark once was located, built themselves a palace. During the 14th and 15th centuries, the heyday of the palace, it housed no less than eight Chancellors of England. After the Reformation, the house fell into disrepair and was later used for commercial purposes until 1814 when a fire destroyed most of the building. All that remained was the western wall of the Great Hall, built in the 14th century, which contained an extra-ordinary fine rose window of the period. For many years all that was visible was the wall and window. But in the more recent developments in the area, the foundations of the hall have been exposed and laid-out for visitors to conceive of its greatness in earlier times. Thanks to Eagle Star the insurance company, a full programme of excavation was carried out and the results left on permanent view for members of the public to visit.

(37) St Mary Overie's Dock.

Another of the ancient hithes of London where, since the 16th century parishioners of the Parish of St Saviour's Southwark have been entitled to land goods free of toll. The suffix "Overie" is said to have derived from either "over the river", or from the ferryman who plied for hire here in the12th century, at a time when there was only one bridge across the Thames - London - and when it was considered safer to cross the river by ferry rather than by using the bridge. One of the daughters of the ferryman, wishing to find out the true feelings of his family towards him and his wishes, and to ascertain what one of his daughters would do on his death regarding marrying the man of her choice - that did not meet with his approval - faked his death. His family were so pleased that after having placing him in his coffin and resting it on a pair of trestles in the boat-house, adjourned to the rest of the house and had a party in celebration. This did not please the father as can be well imagined! He promptly left his coffin, still encased in his shroud, and entered the room of the party. The daughter's boy friend seeing what he took to be a ghost entering the room and pointing a ghostly finger towards him, took evasive action. He grabbed the first object that came to hand, an oar, and struck out at the ghost - and killed the ferryman. The family returned the body to the coffin and carried on with the party. However, in remorse for her father's death the daughter founded a nunnery, on the site where now Southwark Cathedral stands, and entered it.

In the Dock today is the Schooner Kathleen & May, owned by the Maritime Trust, built in North Wales in 1900, with a crew of six. Today it is used as an exhibition craft, for which there is an admission charge.

Built into one of the 19th century warehouses is the Old Thameside public house from whose riverside balcony there is an excellent view across the Thames towards the City of London.

The roadway leads round to…

(38) Southwark Cathedral.

Founded originally as the Convent of St Mary Overie, later in the 9th century St Swithun, Bishop of Winchester, moved the nuns to another convent and installed in their place an Abbey of Augustinian Canons. The abbey survived until the time of the Dissolution of the Monasteries in the 16th century. The buildings were then sold to the parishioners of Southwark for £800, who divided the church into a manageable size and either sold off, or let go to decay, the rest of the building. Stow in his "Survay…" of the late 16th century laments on the use of the retro-choir by a baker who had set up his ovens there. The nave was allowed to fall into ruin, with much of the stone being used to repair the roads of the Borough or used in new housing, etc. The prime condition of the medieval portion of the building owes its very existence to George Gwilt who restored the eastern portion in the late 19th century at his own cost. He wanted to rebuild the ruinous nave but the churchwardens and church council would not allow him. His tomb can be seen at the south

east corner of the church. Having served as a parish church from the Dissolution in 1905 the church was raised to the dignity of a cathedral making it the "head" church for the Diocese of Southwark. If the cathedral is open it is well-worth a visit for there is much to see inside the building. But before entering by way of the south west porch, look to the left hand side by the churchyard railing. Here can be seen herring-bone walling from the Roman Villa built here during the 2nd century. Enter the cathedral and walk across to the font. From here can be seen the high altar. The screen erected by Bishop Richard Fox of Winchester is virtually a history book in stone with the figures (all dating from the 20th century) representing the history of the Church at large, as well as the figures of men and women connected with the locality. The area in the retro-choir (behind the altar) is as perfect an example of medieval architecture as can be found anywhere in London or in England. At the eastern end of the nave, on th south side, is a memorial window and a stone memorial to William Shakespeare. In November 1988 H M Queen Elizabeth opened the extensions to the cathedral on the north side of the building, which include a restaurant that is open until 4.30pm Mondays to Saturdays.

Leave the cathedral by way of the South West Doorway. Turn right. Pause at the stone just inside the railings. This is a 19th century copy of one of the marker stones erected in the 16th century when the Lord Mayor of London claimed part of the district to be the South Ward of the City. Continue to walk along Cathedral Street to the rear of the cathedral (North Side).

The dedication stone on the extensions reads "This stone was dedicated by Ronald, Bishop of Southwark, and laid by Howard Frankham, Provost Emeritus 2nd July 1984. Provost David Edwards. Architect Ronald Sims. Stonemason Tom Adamson". It was opened by H M The Queen in November 1988.

Follow the roadway round to the rear of the cathedral. Here can be seen…

(39) Statue of a Roman Soldier.

The work of Alan Collins, it dates from 1988.

Cross the roadway, ascend a short flight of brick steps to the riverside for yet another view of the City of London across the river. Return to the roadway and cross over. Here can be seen…

(40) London Bridge's Memorial.

There are five stones from the last London Bridge on which there are inscriptions that show the designs of the various bridges that have crossed the river at this point.

(41) "The Mudlark" public house.

The signboard of the public houses shows a young boy and a young girl on the bank of the River Thames looking to see what, if anything, they could find in the mud of the bankside. Even today there are people who search the mud-flats at low tide, some with their metal detectors, some just with their bare hands looking for 'finds'. It should be recorded that all finds today must be reported to the Museum of London, who may or may not decide to retain them for their collections. There was another way of mud-larking which took the form of stuffing mud under the barges as they lay at rest by the bankside. This prevented the barges from sliding down into the river, as the tide receded. It was a most dangerous occupation to follow, and a number of deaths are recorded when the barges slipped on those who were mud-larking at the time. The house is a modern building, with a pleasant enclosed area to sit out in during the summer months. Well worth a visit!

Opposite the public house is the home of three Livery Companies of the City of London.

(42) Livery Hall of the Glaziers and Scientific Instruments Makers.

The elder of these two companies is the Glaziers, who are 53rd in Order of Precedence, and who existed in 1368, with Royal Charters dated 1637 and 1685. In keeping with modern trends of technology etc, the Scientific Instruments Makers Company was formed in 1955, granted its own coat of arms the following year, and in 1963 was granted livery status by the Lord Mayor and Aldermen of the City of London. As with many other modern livery companies they were formed to 'foster and promote goodwill in their trade'. Their 'union' with the Glaziers Company came about in 1977 when the two Courts of the Companies decided on a joint venture of 'one hall for two companies'. The Hall and offices are in a refurbished 19th century building. The building is also home to the Worshipful Company of Launderers, a Company, founded in 1960, and achieved a grant of letters patent in 1978. Membership of the Company is strictly restricted to practitioners of the trade.

To the left of "The Mudlark" public house is an archway. Follow the roadway round until a flight of steps is reached. These lead to the approaches of London Bridge. Walk towards the bridge.

(43) London Bridge, view from…

Pause in the centre of the bridge and look up-river in the direction of St Paul's. From here can be seen part of Bankside along which the route has been followed.

Walk on over the bridge to...

(44) Fishmonger's Hall.

The Worshipful Company of Fishmongers existed long before any of its twenty-four charters were given to it, the earliest of which dates from 1272, and the latest from 1937. The former was granted by Edward I, 1239 - 1307, and the latter by George IV, 1895 - 1952. Like most of the other Livery Companies it was formed in order to regulate the trade of fish in and around London. One of the officials appointed by the Company is the Fishmeter who still has the right of examination of all fish coming into London, albeit since the transferring of Billingsgate Fish Market to a new home on the Isle of Dogs, to the east of London, in January 1982. The hall is the fourth one and was opened in 1834, by the side of the former London Bridge. With the building of the present bridge the Hall makes part of an impressive entrance to the city across the Thames.

Cross under the roadway of the approaches to London Bridge, and descend down the steps into Lower Thames Street. Cross over, by the traffic lights crossing by the Parish Church os St Magnus the Martyr. Walk up Fish Street Hill, back to the Monument underground station.

Covent Garden
"My Fair Lady's Estate"

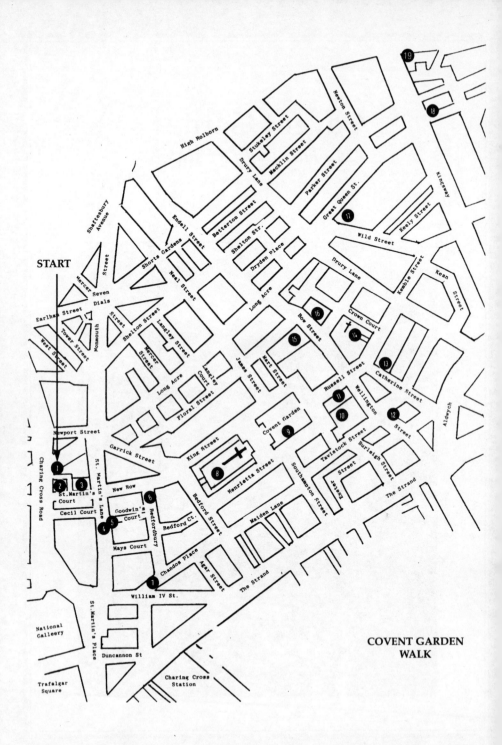

START

COVENT GARDEN
WALK

Key to map

1.   Leicester Square underground station

2.   Wyndhams' Theatre

3.   Albery Theatre

4.   St Martin's Lane

5.   Goodwin's Court

6.   Bedfordbury

7.   Chandos Place

8.   St Paul's Covent Garden Church

9.   Covent Garden

10.   London Transport Museum

11.   Theatre Museum

12.   26, Wellington Street

13.   Theatre Royal, Drury Lane

14.   Crown Court Church

15.   Royal Opera House

16.   Bow Street Police Station

17.   Freemasons' Hall

18.   St Anselm & St Cecilia Catholic Church

19.   Holborn Underground Station

Covent Garden Walk
"My Fair Lady's Estate"

Start: Leicester Square
Underground Station.

Northern and Piccadilly Lines.

Connecting Buses: 24, 29, 176.

Time: allow approximately 2 hours

*L*ong before the famous Covent Garden
Fruit and Vegetable Market was built
here, it was actually founded in 1656 in the
garden of nearby Bedford House, the
monks of Westminster Abbey (Convent)
owned the land here. Until the time of the
Dissolution of the Monasteries in the 16th
century the Benedictine monks of
Westminster tilled the land here for their
own consumption as well as selling off the
surplus to the general public. They even
had their own small chapel close by where
they continued to observe the daily offices
of the Abbey while working in the fields.
Tradition had it that the chapel was later
enlarged and became the first "St Martin
in the Fields" parish church. After the
Dissolution, the area was "granted by the
Crown" to the 1st Earl of Bedford, John
Russell, who commissioned Inigo Jones,
the architect to design a house for himself
and to lay out an estate consisting of a
piazza (square) with surrounding streets
full to capacity of housing. After the
setting up of the Market in the 17th
century, the social status of the area
declined, and, by the 19th century the
market dealt not only in the flower, fruit
and vegetables wares, but also more
general items such as crockery, birds in
their cages, as well as locksmiths and
dealers in "any old iron". Being a private
estate the policing was undertaken by
Beadles of the Bedford Estate, who were
re-inforced later by members of the
Metropolitan Police Force who were hired
in addition to the beadles. When the
Market moved to Nine Elms, Vauxhall, on
the south side of the river, in 1973, the
whole area was re-juvenated and presents
a handsome attraction to the Londoner as
well as the Tourist.

Starting point

(1) Leicester Square underground station.

The station is served by the Piccadilly Line
(1906) and the Northern Line (1907), and takes
its name from the 2nd Earl of Leicester who
built a house nearby in 1637, and later had laid
out Leicester Fields which in turn became
Leicester Square.

Leave the station by way of the exit that
leads to the Wyndhams Theatre.

(2) Wyndhams Theatre.

One of the most consistently successful theatres
of London it was opened in November 1899
having been built for Sir Charles and Lady
Mary (Moore) Wyndham. Early in this
century, the management was taken over by
Frank Curzon and Gerald du Maurier whose
notable productions included "The Dancers" in
which Tallulah Bankhead made her debut on
the London stage. Later Edgar Wallace, 1875-
1932, the very prolific crime writer, dramatist
and journalist, produced a number of his plays
at the theatre. His mother was an actress, his
father an "unknown", Wallace was brought up
by a porter who worked in the Billingsgate Fish
Market, then to be found in Lower Thames
Street, close by St Magnus the Martyr church.

At the side of the theatre is St Martin's
Court walk down the court until St
Martin's Lane is reached. Here can be
seen...

(3) The Albery Theatre.

Another theatre founded and built for Sir
Charles and Lady Wyndham, originally called
The New Theatre in 1903, but later changed to

the Albery in deference to Lady Wyndham's son by her first marriage, Sir Bronson Albery, who became the administrator to the theatre. The theatre has enjoyed a number of "first nights" notably Matheson's "The Wandering Jew" in 1925. Based on the story of a Jew condemned to wander over the world until the second coming of Christ, after having chided Him to walk faster on his way to Calvary. In 1542 Paulus von Eizen, the Bishop of Schleswig met a Jew by the name of Ahasuerus who admitted that he was the "wandering Jew", the story being first published in 1602 in Leyden. The story was later adopted by a number of writers between the 16th and 19th centuries. Goeth wrote a poem about the Jew. In 1925 George Bernard Shaw's "St Joan", with the late Dame Sybil Thorndike in the leading role, was first presented in this theatre. In 1932 the play "Napoleon", written by Mussolini (Il Duce) was performed on the stage here. Robert Atkins played the title role, but the play was not a success! This was a play by a Dictator about a Dictator! In the immediate Post Second World War days, the 1940s, the Old Vic Theatre Company, led by the late Laurence Olivier and Ralph Richardson enchanted audiences with their productions of productions of Shakespearian plays.

In front of the theatre is St Martin's Lane.

(4)   St Martin's Lane.

At the far end of the roadway stands the Parish Church of St Martin in the Fields, the present building being erected by 1726 to the designs of James Gibbs, and the Lane, first built in 1613, can claim many famous persons as its inhabitants. In St Peter's Court, now the site of the Duke of York's Theatre, was once the studio of Roubiliac the sculptor, 1705-1762, after he had been appointed lecturer on sculpture at the St Martin's Lane Academy. The Academy also boasted among its members Hogarth, Reynolds and Mollekins. At number 114 stood the town house of the Earls of Salisbury where, according to tradition, the Seven Bishops were

confined before being committed to the Tower of London. Led by Archbishop Sancroft, 1678-1691, the bishops opposed, 1688, James I's Declaration of Indulgence, which led to their trial on a charge of seditious libel. They were found not guilty by the jury. In the 17th century a number of coffee-houses were established in the Lane, among which was Old Slaughter's which became a popular rendezvous for artists of the time, who, together with the wits and the beaux of the area, enjoyed each other's company. The first Chess Club was founded in the Lane in 1747.

Cross the Lane from the Duke of York's theatre and find...

(5)   Goodwins Court.

First mentioned in the Rate Books for Westminster in 1690 this little piece of Regency London is not to be missed. Here can be seen a delightful row of shop fronts, alas most of them are offices today. Someone once wrote that the windows should be full of old books, but who would find, and buy, them I cannot imagine!

At the far end of the Court, above an archway, is a clock and an old fire insurance mark, is...

(6)   Bedfordbury.

Reminding us of the bury (house) of the Bedford family which stood nearby in the 17th century. Off the street are the Hop Gardens, alleged by MacMichael in his book on the "Story of Charing Cross" to be derived from the fact that Sir Hugh Platt had some experimental gardens here in which he grew hops. Today the street houses the Peabody Buildings. The Estates, and there are a number scattered throughout London, were set up in the 19th century by George Peabody, an American, born 1795, who came to this country where he became a successful stockbroker on the London Stock Exchange.

His plan was to provide living accommodation for workers near their place of work. Many of these estates are today in some of the most expensive areas of London, from the point of view of the value of the land on which they are built - viz. Chelsea, Pimlico and a number of sites in Westminster.

Turn right and walk down Bedfordbury Street until Chandos Place is reached.

(7) Chandos Place.

Named after the 3rd Lord Chandos in 1637, before his death eighteen years later - a rare honour. Here at the hostelry called the Black Prince, Charles Duval, a notorious highwayman, was arrested in 1669. He was hanged at Tyburn and such was his popularity that his body "lay-in-state" within the hour of his execution in the Tangier Tavern in St Giles' Street. The event caused large crowds to gather in the inn, and a judge had to issue an order to them to disperse quietly or suffer the consequences of the action. Surrounded by a body-guard of sturdy men dressed in long black cloaks, his body was taken to the Parish Church of St Paul's, Covent Garden, where it was laid to rest in the central aisle of the building. A white marble stone marked the spot, but this has long since disappeared. According to tradition his bones were later removed and used for anatomy lessons at Surgeon's Hall in the City of London. The epitaph on his tombstone read;

"Here lies DuVall; Reader, if Male thou art, Look to thy purse; if Female, to thy heart. Much havoc has he made of both; for all Men he made stand, and women he made fall. The second Conqueror of the Norman race, Knights to arm arms did yield, and Ladies to his face. Old Tyburn's glory; England's illustrious thief, Du Vall, the Ladies joy; Du Vall, the Ladies grief."

The reference to the Norman race was to the country of his birth, France, where in 1643, he

was born the son of a poor miller from Domfront in Normandy. The hostelry stood at the end of Agar Street, and the site was later to be occupied by the Charing Cross Hospital. A new Charing Cross Hospital was built in Fulham Palace Road to the designs of Ralph Tubbs, and opened in 1973. The Decimus Burton building has been retained and forms the Charing Cross Police Station. Opposite the site of the former hospital, there was a blacking factory shop where the young Charles Dickens used to sit in the window working.

Turn left and walk to the end of Chandos Place, turn left again into Bedford Street, where, a short way up, on the right-hand side of the roadway is Inigo Place. This is the entrance to the church-yard of St Paul's Parish Church, Covent Garden.

(8) Parish Church of St Paul's Covent Garden.

The church was built in 1633 to the designs of Inigo Jones, the architect who introduced the Palladian Style of architecture into England in the 17th century, following a tour of Italy. Andrea Palladio, 1508-1580, was an Italian architect of the late Renaissance whose writings were an enormous influence over English architects of the 17th century. He, in turn, was encouraged in his work by the writings of Vitruvius, an architectural scholar of the First Century BC. His pièce-de-resistance was "De Architectura" which is the only surviving work of its period on architecture and engineering. The book was first published in 1486, with later editions being illustrated. It is said that when the architect asked the Earl of Bedford, on whose estate the church was to be built, what kind of building he favoured, the Earl is alleged to have replied that it should not be much bigger than a barn. "You shall have the handsomest barn in Christendom", Jones replied - and it is! It is a large rectangular building well suited to the time at which it was built, when the sermon dominated the service and the glorious rituals of former times were frowned upon by the clergy and people alike. It was consecrated by the Bishop of London, William Juxon, 1633-1660, in 1633, but was severely damaged by a fire in 1795 and rebuilt - to its original design. In an attempt to convert the 'barn' into a 'church' William Butterfield, 1814-1900, was commissioned in the 19th century to make the necessary changes to the interior of the church. This he did by erecting a platform at the east end of the church, on which the altar stands, and by bricking up the two doorways that led onto the piazza of Covent Garden. Over the past few decades the church has become closely associated with the theatrical world. It is the church of the Actors' Church Union, and the memorials around the inside walls of the church commemorate many a famous actor and actress. In the south wall of the church are entombed the ashes of Ellen Terry, 1847 - 1928, one of the greatest ladies of the English stage and a memorable leading lady of Henry Irving, 1838-1905.

Judy in England and the fact that Samuel Pepys the 17th century diarist witnessed the event. He records in his Diary "9th May 1662. ...Thence to see a Italian puppet play, that is within the rails there - the best I ever saw..." It was also in the portico that George Bernard Shaw set his play "Pygmalion" for Professor Higgins to first meet with Eliza Doolittle. The play was later made into a musical "My Fair Lady" and Covent Garden was 'her estate'. John Wesley, when he preached here in 178? recorded that it was the best constructed church that he had preached in for several years. He also added that a large number of people were turned away from the service, it being full to the brim and overflowing.

Leave the church, and turn left, retracing your steps for a short distance before turning left again into Henrietta Street. Continue to shortly enter Covent Garden.

(9) Covent Garden.

In the centre of what was once the open piazza of Inigo Jones, there now stands the former market buildings designed by Charles Fowler, 1791-1867, who was one of the founders of the Institute of British Architects, that has since received a Royal Charter. The buildings were erected between 1828 and 1831, and formed the centre-piece for the Market area. Following the move of the Market to Vauxhall in 1973 all the buildings were renovated and converted into small units with a number of shops and eating places taking the place of the stalls of the market holders. This whole area has become one of the most popular tourist attractions of the Capital. Before exploring, at your leisure, the many attractive shops, etc, visit the portico of the church where can be seen an inscribed stone recalling the first performance of Punch and

Walk around the shops, etc and then visit in the corner opposite the church.

(10) London Transport Museum.

Here can be seen nearly two hundred years of public transport in London. The Museum is housed in the former Flower Market building of Covent Garden and has on display many examples of the various forms of transport that Londoners have enjoyed over the years. Browse around the exhibits, or drive a train through the underground system, or admire some of the many posters that have invited Londoners, and their visitors, to travel around London and its countryside. There is much to see and enjoy here, and at the end of the visit a coffee shop provides the necessary refreshment to help you on your way.

Leave the entrance to the museum, and turn right, to walk along to Russell Street. Here is to be found another museum.

(11) The Theatre Museum.

The idea for the museum was conceived in 1974, but it took another decade before it came to fruition. Here can be seen "bits and pieces" from theatres from all over the country, as well as semi and permanent displays showing the history and development of the theatre in Britain. Like the Transport Museum it is housed in part of the former Flower Hall of Covent Garden.

Russell Street, in the 18th century, was the home of Buttons Coffee House which was a favourite gathering point for men of the theatre to meet and 'talk shop'. In 1713 Joseph Addison, 1672-1719, dramatist, poet, and essayist, installed a letter box here for contributions to the "Guardian" and the "Tatler" publications. In was in the shape of a lion's mouth through which the letters were posted! Buttons' successor was the Bedford Coffee House in the piazza, in the north east corner, which has been described as being "a place of resort of the critics… everyone you meet is a polite scholar and critic… the merit of every production of the press is weighed and determined…"

Russell Street leads to Wellington Street. Turn right until Wellington Street is crossed by Tavistock Street.

(12) 26 Wellington Street.

On the corner of Tavistock Street were the offices of "All the year round", a weekly publication founded in 1859 by Charles Dickens, 1812 - 1870, which he continued to edit until his death. It was the successor of "Household Words" which he had started in 1850. Here he set up bachelor quarters for himself where he gave a number of readings during the London Season.

Turn left into Tavistock Street and then turn left again into Catherine Street.

A short distance on the right can be seen…

(13) The Theatre Royal, Drury Lane.

The first theatre on the site was opened in May 1663, with a play by Beaumont and Fletcher "The Humerous Lieutenant", while the stage was graced with the presence of Nell Gwyn 1650 - 1687, in 1665 who appeared in John Dryden's, 1631 - 1700, play "The Indian Emperor". Fire destroyed the first theatre, which was replaced in 1670 by a building designed by Sir Christopher Wren, 1632-1723, which in turn was replaced by another building in 1794. Meanwhile the management had to be taken over by Richard Sheridan, 1751 - 1816, in 1776, who produced a number of his own plays here. It was during Sheridan's reign that the theatre was rebuilt for the fourth time, again after a disastrous fire had wrecked the building by which time Sheridan had become a Member of Parliament, and, on hearing that his theatre was on fire, left the House of Commons and watched the fire burn from a hostelry opposite. When a passer-by commented on the fact he replied "Cannot a man have a quiet drink by his own fireside". In 1812 the present building was opened, the fifth on the site, with an address by Lord Byron, 1788 - 1824, which was followed by a performance of Shakespeare's "Hamlet". In recent years the theatre has been associated with a series of highly successful musical productions.

To the side of the theatre is Russell Street, off of which is Crown Court here is to be found…

(14) Crown Court Church.

Taking its name from the Crown Tavern, the court is the home of the National Scottish Church which was founded for Scots living in London prior to unification of the Kingdoms of Scotland and England in the early 17th century. At that time it was centred around

Scotland Yard at the northern end of Whitehall. The present building, by Messrs Balfour and Turner was erected earlier in this century and is in the Neo-Elizabethan style of architecture. The church is open to visitors during the summer months, and on Sundays, for services throughout the rest of the year.

At the end of Crown Court is Broad Court turning left leads you into Bow Street.

(15) Royal Opera House, Covent Garden, Bow Street.

John Rich founded a theatre here which was opened in December 1732 with the play "The Way of the World" by Congreve, 1670 - 1729. The cost of the theatre , £6,000, was raised by public subscription, with an annual ground rent of £100. The measure of the success of the project can be gauged by the fact that by 1792 the ground rent was raised to £940 per year. As a theatre, as opposed to an opera house, it can make a number of claims to fame. Oliver Goldsmith, 1728 - 1774, wrote "She stoops to conquer" attended the first night here in 1773, while Richard Sheridan's "The Rivals" was also first presented here in 1775. In September 1808 disaster struck when fire destroyed the theatre and twenty-three firemen were killed in the blaze. The loss was assessed as being £150,000 only half of which was covered by insurance. A year later a new theatre was opened, with the popular Shilling Gallery being abolished and all the other seats costing considerably more than previously. There were riots in the theatre, with chanting taking place during the productions demanding the return of the Gallery and of the old prices. The objectors won the day and all was restored. Again, in 1856, fire destroyed the theatre the ruins of which became a popular pastime to visit. Even Queen Victoria and Prince Albert came to see for themselves the extent of the damage. After this, the present building was erected to the designs of Sir Edward Barry, 1830 - 1880, who was the third son of Sir Charles Barry, 1795 - 1860, the architect of

Westminster Palace (the Houses of Parliament). Since this time the theatre has been devoted to the Opera and Ballet, and in 1939 was named the Royal Opera House. The interior of the theatre is suitably adorned in the rich colours of red and gold, with an extension, built in 1982, housing rehearsal rooms, and further work is currently on the way for more improvements.

Opposite the Royal Opera House is...

(16) Bow Street Magistrates' Court and Police Station.

Law and order have been resident in Bow Street since 1749 when a court was set up here by Colonel De Veil in his house at No 4. The famous Bow Street Runners, founded by Henry Fielding, after he considered the work of the parish constables was ineffective, started as a volunteer body of some six to eight men. Part-timers they were allowed a share of the reward money, and could also be hired by private individuals seeking protection for themselves and their homes. Not wearing a uniform they were able to mix with the general populace and so did not frighten away any would-be felon. The Runners were not disbanded until 1839, some ten years after the Metropolitan Police Act was placed on the Statute Book. After one of her many visits to the Opera House Queen Victoria sent a letter to the Police Station objecting to the colour of the lamp which hung outside the station - it was blue! Bow Street Police Station was the only one with a white light suspended over the front door of the building. The work of the police station has now been transferred to the Charing Cross Police Station.

Facing the Royal Opera House turn right up Bow Street to Long Acre. Turn right to soon enter Great Queen Street which is dominated by...

(17) Freemasons' Hall.

Opened in 1933 by the Duke of Connaught, the grand Master of the English Masons, it was first called the Masonic Peace Memorial and commemorated the many masons who were killed in the First World War, 1914 - 1918. Designed by H V Ashley and F Winton Newman, it stands on the site of the Freemasons' Arms public house which in turn was replaced by Sandby's Hall of 1775. A new Freemasons' Hall was built in the latter half of the 19th century by Francis Pepys Cockerell, only a small part of this, and its previous building remains today, and these have been incorporated into the Connaught Rooms. The Present Hall includes a Grand Temple, library, museum, as well as a number of smaller rooms that can be used for Masonic purposes.

At the end of Great Queen Street turn left and cross over the roadway - Kingsway to the Catholic Church of St Anselm & St Cecilia.

(18) Catholic Church of St Anselm & St Cecilia.

The construction of Kingsway between The Strand and High Holborn has been described a one of the greatest of the road improvement schemes of the late 19th century. Begun in 1892 and costing circa £5,000,000, it was opened in 1905 by Edward VII, 1841 - 1910, when, it is said, he forgot the words of his speech and had to be prompted! During the work, the former Catholic Church was demolished and the present one built. Inside there is an altar from the previous church which had served the Sardinian Embassy nearby, and one from the Lady Chapel at Glastonbury. On the occasion of the last Mass in the old church all the congregation "knelt and kissed the floor" before leaving.

From the church it is a short walk to **(19)** Holborn underground station which is served by both Piccadilly and Central Lines.

East of Aldgate

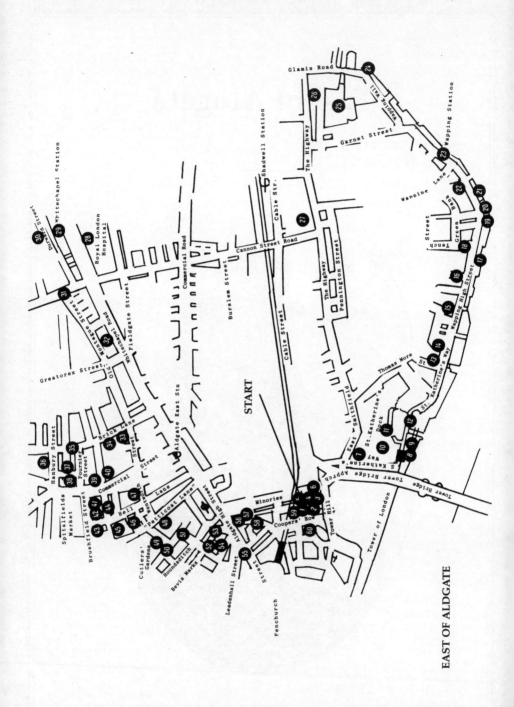

EAST OF ALDGATE

Key to map

1. Tower Hill Underground Station
2. Tower Hill Underground Station - booking hall
3. Sundial
4. Statue of Emperor Trajan
5. Roman Funeral Inscription
6. Postern Gate Remains
7. World Trade Centre
8. Girl with The Dolphin Fountain
9. Timepiece
10. Coronarium Chapel
11. Ivory House
12. Marine Club
13. Thomas More Street Sign
14. London Dock's Lock
15. Hermitage Court
16. Peirhead Houses
17. Town of Ramsgate Public House
18. Scandrett Street
19. Metropolitan Police Boatyard
20. Riverside Gardens
21. Wapping Police Station
22. Tower Buildings
23. Wapping Underground Station
24. Prospect of Whitby Public House
25. Shadwell Basin
26. St Paul's Parish Church, Shadwell
27. Parish Church of St George in the East
28. Royal London Hospital
29. Whitechapel Underground Station
30. Bucks Row (now Durward Street)
31. Old Montague Street
32. Hopetown
33. Spitalfields Health Centre
34. Christchurch School
35. Mosque
36. Hanbury Street - courtyard
37. Wilkes Street
38. Puma Court
39. The Ten Bells Public House
40. Parish Church of Christchurch Spitalfields
41. The London Fruit Exchange
42. The London Wool Exchange
43. The Gun Public House
44. Private roadway
45. Roman Catholic Convent
46. Artillery Lane
47. Bell Lane Housing Estate
48. "Petticoat Lane"
49. Former bonded warehouse
50. Cutler Street
51. White Kennet Street
52. Great Synagogue Plaque
53. Sir John Cass Church of England Primary School
54. Mitre Square
55. Aldgate Pump
56. Jewry Street
57. "Sir John Cass College"
58. Crutched Friars Statues
59. City Wall
60. Trinity House

East of Aldgate

Start: Tower Hill Underground Station.

Circle and District Lines.

Connecting buses: 15, 25, 42, 78.

Time: allow approximately 3 hours.

*I*t was Henry Mayhew's "London Labour and the London Poor" whose first three volumes were published in 1851, the year of the Great Exhibition in Hyde Park, that drew attention to the continuing plight of those Londoners who lived, worked and died - to the East of Aldgate. In 1902, after six months extensive research, the American author Jack London published "The People of the Abyss" that, once again, revealed the social and economic horrors of London's East End. Everywhere there was evidence of violence, fighting between friends and neighbours seeking to find employment. Murders were an almost nightly event. People lived in the most horrific and crowded circumstances. Prostitutes were to be found on every street-corner. The streets were ill-lit, if at all, and in many a dark alley there lurked danger of some kind or other. The only people about after dark were up to no good, or were rushing between home and their place of work.

London has always, and still does, attract refugees from all over the world. In the seventeenth century the Huguenots came from France fleeing from persecution by the government. Later the Italians arrived for a similar reason. They all settled "just outside the City Wall", they all made their contribution to London in one way or other. But there was precious little accommodation for them all. Hence the over crowding and in those circumstances others were also drawn to live here - the undesirables, the vagrants, the homeless from other parts, and not least the criminals. All could, and did, find refuge here. Lost in the ever growing crowds of people.

Before the Second World War the Chinese had arrived in their droves and settled around Limehouse. Here they created their own China Town until during the last war, when much of their property was destroyed. Everybody knew the way to China Town but few could remember where Limehouse was to be found! After 1945 they sought to rebuild their lives, their houses and their shops but found that times had changed. Now, they have built themselves a New China Town in London's West End. Visit Gerrard Street and see how they have adapted to a new life in a new place.

The Blitz of 1940 - 1941 hit the East End very hard, but it could not, and did not, break the hearts of the people. After the conflict was over work soon started to rebuild the ruins of war. Many of the poorer houses were rebuilt and replaced by blocks of flats, and large housing estates sprung up all over the area. Today, as in the past, the area's population reflects the movement of people from many other countries to Britain. They all make up the kaleidoscope of the land beyond Aldgate.

Starting point:

(1) Tower Hill Underground Station

Leave the station by way of the Exit whose opening hours are:

Mondays to Fridays	7am to 8pm
Saturdays	7am to 7pm
Sundays	8am to 7pm.

At other times the Exit is through the booking hall nearby (2). Outside the station there is a mound on top of which there is a...

(3) Sundial.

The sundial has illustrations around its perimeter telling the story of London. From here there is a good view of the Tower of London. In one corner is an engraved plate showing the principal buildings around Tower Hill.

Leave the mound by way of the stairs, at the foot turn right. Descend the steps that lead to the booking office of the station. But at the half-way landing turn left into the open space in front of the City Wall. Here can be seen...

(4) The statue of the Roman Emperor Trajan.

The work of an Italian sculptor. It was discovered in a scrapyard by the late Revd. "Tubby" Clayton, Founder of the Toc H Movement, on a visit to Southampton. The Tower Hill Improvement Trust erected it here in 1980 as part of the landscaping of the garden.

(5) Built into the wall to the left of the statue is a copy of London's oldest funeral inscriptions. It records the burial nearby of Caius Iulius Alpinus Classicianus of the Fabian Tribe... Procurator of the Province of Britain... Iulia Pacata daughter of... Indus his sorrowing wife. Unfortunately, to date, only the top and the bottom portions of the stone have been recovered. It is believed that the missing section recalls his career in the Roman Empire. Research has revealed that Classicianus was almost certainly the successor of Decianus Catus who was responsible for the uprising by Queen Boudicea after the ravaging of her daughters.

Complete the walk down the steps. Ahead is a short tunnel that leads to the Tower of London. At the end of the tunnel can be seen...

(6) The ruins of the City's Postern Gate.

Built in the 13th century. Note in particular the narrow (arrow) windows that enabled the archer to shoot out at an enemy, but the narrowness of the window made it very difficult for the attacker to kill the archer within.

Turn and walk to the left - along the walkway above the moat of the Tower. Here too are gardens for the weary to rest in, or for others to ponder on their next place to visit. At the end of the walkway there are steps that lead to Tower Bridge, but we continue along the tunnel at the end of which we turn to the right and walk through the gardens in front of the World Trade Centre **(7)**. After crossing over two small bridges step to the left between the buildings to look over into the Dock at the many fine boats and barges which are moored there.

(7) Around the World Trade Centre

Here are the remains of the 19th century warehouses that once stood on this site. The area between the World Trade Centre and International House has been made into an amphitheatre.

Returning to the path once more continue to walk towards the river.

The buildings here have all been rebuilt since the bombing of the last War, and are, today, occupied by offices and a restaurant. At the end of this stretch of St Katharine's Way is the River Thames. Here can be seen, looking under bridge, a fine view of the Upper Pool of London, H.M.S. Belfast and London Bridge. Signs on the riverside wall read "French Boules' is played here".

Turn left and walk along the riverside. Shortly there can be seen...**(8)** The Girl with The Dolphin Fountain by David Wynne. Erected in 1973. Continue along the riverside, past the Tower Hotel pier from where one can board the river bus and under the hotel until **(9)** is reached.

(9) *"Timepiece" by Wendy Taylor, 1973, is made of stainless and forged steel and bronze.*

Cross over the lock of St Katharine's Dock where twice a day, when the tide of the river allows, boats are let in or out of the dock. Shortly after crossing the bridge on the side wall there is a replica of the Saint Katharine-by-the-Tower seal. Next to it a plaque recalls the visit to the dock by H M Queen Beatrix of the Netherlands. Ahead lies the former dock, now marina, of St Katharine. From this position it is possible to see…

(10) *The circular inter-denominational chapel - the Coronarium Chapel.*

Ahead can be seen…

(11) *Ivory House.*

Completed in 1854 to the designs of George Aitcheson the Younger with cast iron columns and attractive brickwork above. Built to house

the Ivory Trade's wares there are shops and restaurants at ground level., and the upper space has been converted into comfortable living quarters, all of which overlook the marina.

(The walker may like to make a diversion at this point of the walk and explore more deeply St Katharine's of the twentieth century) The walk continues by walking along St Katharine's Way, leave the dock area from in front of the Marine Club **(12)**.

The roadway is lined on either side by buildings from the last two centuries, with former warehouses being converted into luxury flats or apartments. On the left hand side of the road can be seen a housing estate built by the former London County Council in the 1930s.

At the end of Thomas More Street **(13)** there is a sign pointing toward Tobacco Dock and the Pirate Ships, just beyond which is the former lock for the London Docks **(14)** that have been filled in.

Continue to walk along St Katharine's Way until just after Hermitage Court **(15)** on the left hand side of the road. Here cross over the road to…

Wapping Docks

*Wapping Docks entrance lock and the Pierhead Houses dating from 1811 - 1812. The lock has long since been filled in and provides a front garden for the houses **(16)**. Ahead is the Town of Ramsgate Public House **(17)** at the side of which there is a passage, Old Wapping Stairs, leading down to the river. Here can be seen a modern, unused, gibbet its predecessor being used to hang pirates and the like for crimes committed at sea. It was on these steps that Bloody Judge Jeffries - the hanging judge - was discovered hidden in a laundry basket waiting to be smuggled aboard ship. He was taken to the Tower of London, where he wasted away, and was later buried in an unmarked grave in the former Parish Church of St Mary*

Aldermanbury, near the Guildhall in the City of London. The public house, well-worth a visit, with the riverside patio available for children, takes its present name from the fishermen of Ramsgate, in Kent. Tradition says that they

used to anchor their fishing boats alongside the 'pub after taking their catch to be sold at the Billingsgate Fish Market near London Bridge. Some books record that the public house was formerly known as "The Red Cow" in deference to the colour of the hair of a popular barmaid. Tradition has a lot to answer for!!

After your visit to the Town of Ramsgate or Wapping Old Stairs cross the road to ...

(18) Scandrett Street.

Here can be seen the ruins of St John's Parish Church and its school, dating from 1790, they were both heavily bombed during the Second World War and have not been restored. Although the tower with its, working, clock have received attention, there are no plans currently to fully restore either or both of the buildings.

Where Scandrett Street joins Trench Street turn into Green Bank. On one side of the road is a pleasant recreation ground and on the other the Roman Catholic Church of St Patrick. At the far end of the church building is Dundee Street. Turn right, walk along and rejoin Wapping High Street at the other end. Turn left and cross the road. Here can be seen the Metropolitan Police Boatyard that services the river police **(19)**.

Next to the boatyard building is a pleasant riverside garden **(20)** from where one can enjoy a splendid view of the river and in the near distance the tall tower office block of the Canary Wharf Development. Across the river can be seen The Angel public house "a sixteenth century riverside pub". Samuel Pepys records in his Diary visiting the pub having walked over the fields from the Naval Dockyards at Deptford.

On leaving the garden turn right and walk to the nearby Wapping Police Station **(21)**.

(21) Wapping Police Station.

When the original station was erected in 1797 it was to house the first River Police patrol in the world. The present, twentieth century building is the home of the Thames Division of the Metropolitan Police who still patrol the river.

Opposite the station is another "oasis" of grass and space for the children to play in safely. Next to the gardens is Tower Buildings **(22)** a nineteenth century block of apartments. On the other side can be seen a well restored building in which has been built "The Captain Kidd" public house.

Kidd was a notorious sea captain who was commissioned in 1696 to suppress pirates but instead joined them! He was finally caught in New England and sent back to London where in 1701 he was hanged at Executive Dock close to Wapping Old Stairs.

From here it is a short walk to...

(23) Wapping Underground Station.

The Station was originally opened in 1869 as Wapping & Shadwell and renamed Wapping in 1876. The world's first underwater tunnel, linking Wapping with Rotherhithe on the opposite side of the river, was opened in March 1843 - as a tunnel for foot passengers.

Designed by Isambard Brunel it was intended to be used by vehicular traffic but there was insufficient money available to build the necessary ramps. In the 1860s it was bought by the East London Railway Company and converted into a tunnel for use by its trains. A visit to Rotherhithe by train makes a pleasant diversion. At platform level the twin horse-shoe shaped tunnels can be seen while the journey along the 1,200 foot tunnel only takes a few minutes. (Rotherhithe was one of a number of villages engaged in ship building in former days. The Parish Church of St Mary's was rebuilt in the eighteenth century. Captain Christopher Jones, Master of the Mayflower that carried the Pilgrim Fathers to New England lies buried in the churchyard. Nearby is the "Mayflower Public House" that has been the centre of parish life since the sixteenth century when it was called "The Shippe". Tradition relates that when the house was restored in the following century some of the timbers from the "Mayflower" were used.)

The walk continues, on the north bank of the river along Wapping High Street past the various blocks of flats some of which have been converted from 19th century, warehouses. By New Crane Wharf the roadway bends to the left and shortly afterwards can be seen the former "Three Suns" public house, with its terracotta decoration on the facade of the building. The next corner marks the beginning of Wapping Wall. Turn right and passing the warehouses on the right hand side and the new houses on the left the "Prospect of Whitby" public house **(24)** is reached.

(24) "Prospect of Whitby"

On the front of the building there is a sign claiming the house to be the oldest pub on the riverside. It was originally built in 1520, during the reign of Henry VIII, at which time the house was surrounded by fields and marshland - but not so today. Due to its previous clientele often being river pirates and

smugglers the house was given the name "The Devil's Tavern". By the 19th century the name had changed to its present one, the change coming about by the mooring of a fishing smack called "The Prospect" that was registered at Whitby, Yorkshire. Charles Dickens in his novel "Our Mutual Friend" uses the house and renames it the "Six Jolly Fellowship Porters".

Continue to walk towards the bridge over the entrance to the ...

(25) Shadwell Basin.

Built as part of the extensions to London Dock in the mid-nineteenth century the Basin is now surrounded by modern housing and the water of the dock used for leisure purposes.

Before walking over the bridge visit the open space on the left hand side and see the modern development and use of this former dock. Over the bridge is Glamis Road, and at the end is The Highway. Turn left and walk along to...

(26) St Paul's Parish Church, Shadwell.

A chapel-at-ease was first built here in 1656, but with the increase in the population later in the same century (1660) it was rebuilt and became the Parish Church of Shadwell. During the eighteenth century the church became known as the Sea Captains' Church from the many sea captains whose names appear in the Parish Registers between 1730 and 1790. Captain James Cook, the circum-navigator of the world's, son was born here. His family at that time were living at 88 Mile End Road where a "blue-plaque" on the wall commemorates the event.

Walk along The Highway until a traffic light crossing. Cross over the roadway and walk towards ...

(27) The Parish Church of St George in the East.

One of the proposed Fifty New Churches to be built in and around London in the early eighteenth century. The Fund was financed by the Coal Tax of 1711, and although the original plan was to build or rebuild fifty churches, only a dozen were ever completed. Designed by Nicholas Hawksmoor its solid stone lantern still dominates the skyline of the area. During the Second World War the interior was badly damaged, and for a time a wooden hut was erected in the nave of the church for use by the parishioners. Between 1960 and 1964 the church was restored, but, not to its former state. Instead the architect Arthur Bailey built inside the walls a church that occupies half the original building. He excavated the large crypt, the coffins were removed and re-buried elsewhere, turning the area into a large parish hall. Also within the walls are flats and offices for use of the Rector and his staff. The west wall of the new church is made up of large glass panels. The whole church is visible through the former west doorway at night from Cannon Street Road when the altar is spotlit.

From the church turn right and walk along Canon Street Road to Commercial Road passing on the way Cable Street, once the haunt of seamen, "ladies of easy virtue" and some very poor housing. Today all these have been replaced by modern housing estates. Cross over Commercial Road and continue to walk along New Road. At the end of the road is Whitechapel Road. Turn right. Shortly after on the right can be seen the...

(28) Royal London Hospital

The hospital has a helipad on the roof of the Alexandra Wing. A group of seven gentlemen meeting in the "Feather Tavern" in the City's Cheapside set in motion the setting up of a new hospital. By 1757 it had outgrown the original house in Moorfields and alternative premises had to be built. Two years later this building,

rated to be the finest of its kind in 1759, was open for use. At first there was strong resistance to turn the establishment into a teaching hospital on the grounds that they were there to heal the poor and not for the purpose of teaching. However, towards the end of the eighteenth century and at the insistence of William Blizzard "one of the outstanding medical men of the century", a one storey building was erected to house such a Medical School. Much damaged in the Second World War it has now recovered and functions as well as ever in its long history.

Cross the road by way of the traffic light crossing immediately in front of the main entrance to the hospital. But before crossing look towards Whitechapel Underground Station **(29)**.

(29) Whitechapel Underground Station.

The building to the right of the station entrance was, a hundred years ago a public house and was used as a resting place for Mary Anne Nichols's body before it was taken to the mortuary. Who was Anne Mary Nichols? She was the first victim of the person who came to be known as "Jack The Ripper".

To the right of the crossing there is an archway bearing a sign "Wood's Buildings". Pass under the arch and walk through to the other end of the passage and over the bridge that crosses the platforms of Whitechapel Station. At the end descend the short flight of steps, turn left, and walk round to the right. Pause.

(30) Bucks Row and Murder

Here was Bucks Row, later Durward Street, where in the early hours of 31st August 1888 P.C. Neil's attention was drawn to a bundle of clothes lying in the gutter. She had been murdered. So began a reign of terror that was to last from late August to early November in

1888. Nobody to this day is absolutely sure "Who-dunnit". Names, some famous, have been bandied about in police circles - but nobody, but nobody has ever been charged and found guilty of those heinous crimes. It is unlikely that anybody will ever be firmly accused and/or found guilty. Such was the cover-up of these events.

The area today has completely changed from a hundred years ago, and there are more plans to develop and improve the living accommodation for the people who live in the area. Turn away and walk towards the other end of Durward Street. Here is Vallance Road. Turn right and walk along to the pedestrian crossing and cross over the roadway. On reaching the other side bear to the left and through Old Montague Street (31).

Old Montague Street is lined with flats and Houses forming part of a modern housing estate.

Cross Greatorex Street. Shortly afterwards there is the Salvation Army Social Services' Hopetown (32).

(32) Hopetown.

In 1931 the late Queen Mary visited Stepney to open a new Salvation Army hostel for needy women. It was called Hopetown. The local Borough of Stepney's Councillors were so impressed by the Royal visit, and by the work of the Army that they renamed one of the streets. The present building is a replacement of the one opened by the late Queen.

At the end of the street turn right into Brick Lane. Here can be seen...

(33) *at Nos 9 to 11, the Spitalfields Health Centre, designed by Shepheard Epstein & Hunter with J S Allen. It was opened in 1984.*

(34) Christchurch School.

A Church of England Primary School. The

stone plaque on the side wall reads "Christ Church Middlesex. This house and these schools were erected in AD 1873 in lieu of the house and parochial schools as shown above that formerly stood in the north west corner of the churchyard of this parish."

(35) Mosque.

On the corner of Brick Lane and Fournier Street stands an eighteenth century building that has been in its time a Catholic Church, Non-Conformist Chapel, Synagogue and is now a Mosque. The change of use reflects the change of population of this area.

Walk along the Lane to Hanbury Street. Turn left.

(36) No. 29 Hanbury Street, another murder.

Here in the courtyard (36) of No 29 on 8th September 1888 Annie Chapman was murdered by the Ripper. It is likely that he 'picked her up' at the nearby "Ten Bells Public House", and that she could have identified him had she been allowed to live. But she wasn't. Today the site of the house and courtyard is covered by the Truman Brewery buildings. The design by Arup Associates won three major architectural awards, and was complimented for its incorporation of the eighteenth century Brewer House on the site.

Leading off Hanbury Street on the left hand side is Wilkes Street (37). A walk down here will give some insight into the seventeenth century style of domestic architecture. On the right hand side of the street is...

(38) Puma Court.

On the right hand side of which is Norton Folgate House. The stone engraved inscription reads "These almshouses were erected in the year of 1860 for poor inhabitants of the Liberty of Norton Folgate in place of those built in

1728 lately pulled down for the new street". Opposite the almshouses are three shops dating from the early nineteenth century - and they are still in use.

At the end of the Court turn left into Commercial Street. Walk along to the next corner where stands...

(39) "The Ten Bells" Public House.

The pub, previously known as "The Jack the Ripper", and where it seems likely that Annie Chapman met The Ripper. The walls inside the house have reproductions of the Illustrated Police Weekly telling of the deeds of The Ripper with drawings of the victims.

(40) *The Parish Church of Christchurch Spitalfields stands on the other corner of Fournier Street. This is another of the Fifty Churches Act of the eighteenth century and was designed by Nicholas Hawksmoor. Note the engraved stone on the Fournier Street side informing the passer-by, and others who may wish to make use of the information there, that the parish fire engine's shed key is available from the Parish Clerk.*

Cross the road and walk along Brushfield Street on the left hand side, where can be found...

(41) The London Fruit Exchange and (42) The London Wool Exchange

Both of which are housed in a building that was opened by the Lord Mayor of London, Sir John E K Studd, in 1929.

On the corner of Brushfield Street and Crispin Street is...

(43) "The Gun" Public House.

On the side of the house a board proclaims "The fields of the parish of St Mary Spital were open space outside the City Wall, and used

mainly for recreational purposes. Henry VIII granted a Royal Warrant to the Honourable Artillery Company in 1537, and later gave them permission to practice in Spital Fields. "The Gun" takes its name from the artillery barracks established near Artillery Lane. Because of the influence of the Huguenots who settled in the area, the barracks became known as the French Barracks.

Walk down Crispin Street and shortly there will appear on the left hand side a private road **(44).**

Shown on nineteenth century maps as Dorset Street with, Miller's Court, the home of Mary Kelly off to the left. This was the Ripper's last and only indoor murder. Mary's body was found the next day, 9th November 1888, by the rent collector who smelt burning and let himself in by putting his hand through the broken glass of the door.

On the opposite side of Crispin Street is the...

(45) Roman Catholic Convent.

The convent is where Annie Chapman had spent the night before she met The Ripper. It was probably the need for a few pence for "bed and breakfast" here that she went with him. The convent still today offers beds to the homeless and the vagrants with separate dormitories for men and women. They each have their own entrance doors on different sides of the building.

Off Crispin Street to one side of the convent is Artillery Lane **(46).**

(46) Artillery Lane.

Here can be seen two superbly restored eighteenth century shops with rooms above and close by is Artillery Passage giving twentieth century visitors an insight into the many side streets that existed in Medieval London. One has only to imagine a building on one side of the Passage catching fire, falling forward, and so igniting the rest of the buildings.

Return to Crispin Street and Bell Lane at the junction of these two roadways on the right hand side is Frying Pan Alley. The derivation of its name has caused concern to many a street names researcher. Hector Bolitho and Derek Peel in "Without the City Wall" write "we walked on to Frying Pan Alley... and left as bewildered as ever by the name..." Perhaps it was the name of a long lost inn or tavern. Or were the tinkers here mending pots and pans?

Walk down Bell Lane, noting on the way the 1930s London County Council's housing estate (47). These were part of a plan to demolish the former nineteenth century houses and replace them with up-to-date housing for the people of the East End of London. The Second World War stopped the plan from proceeding and the area had to wait nearly a quarter of a century before seeing neighbouring buildings brought up to standard.

Cross Cobb Street and at Wentworth Street turn right and walk ahead to Middlesex Street.

(48) Petticoat Lane.

Middlesex Street is better known as "Petticoat Lane" and is famous for its Sunday Market. In former times the main items sold here were the petticoats of the ladies and other pieces of underwear. Middlesex Street marks the boundary between the City of London and the former County of Middlesex. Note the different style of the lampposts on either side of the roadway. Here one side of the street comprises the City of London's housing estate Petticoat Square a Post-War Development, the other retains its pre-war look.

At Harrow Way turn left.

Until the 1970s the buildings on the right hand side were Bonded Warehouses (49). Since that time they have been converted by Richard Seifert & Partners, architects, into a small complex of offices and shops. The entrance is in Cutler Street (50), and well worth a diversion to stroll around the courtyards.

The walk continues along White Kennett Street (51), turn right into Stoney Lane. Another street name that is hard to be certain of its origin, possibly from the fact that it was paved with stone which was a rare feature of earlier times. At the end of the Lane cross over Houndsditch, the site of the City Wall's ditch where in former times rubbish was dumped - including dead dogs. Turn left on the other side of the roadway and walk down Creechurch Lane. Walk along to...

(52) The Great Synagogue.

A plaque reads "The Great Synagogue Duke's Place a constituent of the United Synagogue stood on the site adjoining from 1890 and served the community continuing until it was destroyed September 1941 in World War Two".

On the corner of St Jame's Place is the Sir John Cass Church of England Primary School.

(53) Sir John Cass C of E Primary School.

Built to the designs of A W Cooksey in 1908 it is the school's third building having been founded in 1669 by Zachary Crofton in Houndsditch. It later moved to Old Jewry 1869, after being closed for a number of years. In 1895 a new Trust was set up enabling the school to build new premises here. The site of St Jame's Church, Duke's Place, is now the school playground. The Passage being a reminder of the church built within the precinct of the Priory of the Holy Trinity. Declared redundant in 1874 the church was demolished and its raredos (carved screen behind the altar) erected in the Church of St Katharine Creechurch.

At the end of the Passage is Mitre Square **(54)**.

(54) Mitre Square.

The square marks the site of the cloisters of the Priory of the Holy Trinity, founded in 1108 by Matilda of Scotland the wife of Henry I, for the Canons of St Augustine. John Stow in his "Survay of the Cities of London and Westminster" 1598, writes "this priory, in the process of time, became a very fair and large church, rich in lands and ornaments, and passed all the priories in the City of London or shore of Middlesex". Evidence of its importance can be seen reflected by noting the appointment of the prior as an alderman of the City. Thereby being able to take part in the government of the City. In the corner of the square is a raised flower bed with a wooden bench for the walker to sit and meditate on the past history of the site, or simply to rest.

Mitre Square is also where another victim of The Ripper was found. In the early morning of 30th September 1888 a police constable stumbled over the body of Catherine Eddows a well-known prostitute from "East of Aldgate". She had been released from the Bishopsgate Police Station some time after midnight and was making her way home through the back streets of the City. Here she met The Ripper and was murdered.

Mitre Street runs along one side of the square, at the end of the street there is a junction of three important streets of the City, viz. Aldgate, Fenchurch and Leadenhall Streets. At the end of Mitre Street turn right, cross the roadway by the traffic lights to...

(55) The Aldgate Pump.

Mention of a pump nearby to the present one was recorded in the reign of King John (1199-1216) when it is shown as 'a well called Alegate". Following alterations to widen the roadways in the 1860s the pump was moved to its present position. Following a series of complaints about the taste of the water towards the end of the nineteenth century checks were made to its source. During the course of investigations it was discovered that the underground stream that fed the well passed through several graveyards or cemeteries. It was the calcium from the bones in the water that gave it that "extra taste". Since 1876 the pump has been supplied by fresh water from the New River Company's supply. The brass wolf's head that fed the well pump is said to be a memorial for the last wolf to be shot in the City of London.

Cross over the end of Fenchurch Street. Turn left and walk to Jewry Street **(56)**. Here can be seen...

(57) Sir John Cass College.

*Founded in 1710 the Sir John Cass College of Science and Technology which became the first school of Science in London. Today the premises are occupied by the City of London University. At the junction of Jewry Street and Crutched Friars and on the corner of Rangood Street **(58)** stands the statues of two crutched friars by Michael Black. They are made of red Swedish Granite with an off-white marble for the heads and hands. The Order of the Holy Cross was founded in London in 1298 and moved here in the fourteenth century when they were given land by Messrs Ralph Hosiar and William Sabernes. The friars wore a habit (clothes) at first grey and later it changed to blue, over their outer garments they wore a red (leather) cross. Hence they became known as the Crossed or Crutched Friars. Dissolved at the time of the Dissolution of the Monasteries in 1539 their land was bought by Sir Thomas Wyatt who built himself a mansion on part of the site. The refectory (dining hall) of the Friary was converted into a glass conservatory - the first in England.*

Ahead can be seen the railway bridge of Fenchurch Street Station under which passes Coopers' Row.

Here on the left hand side through an arched office building is a very fine stretch of the City Wall **(59)**. The public are allowed near to the wall to inspect it. Look over the balustrade and see the Roman foundations to the City Wall and the later, medieval, portions that were built on to it.

Return to Coopers's Row and so to Trinity Square **(60)** where the north side is dominated by Trinity House the guardians of the coasts of England and Wales.

From Trinity Square it is only a short walk to Tower Hill Underground Station.

Marylebone
In search of Sherlock Holmes

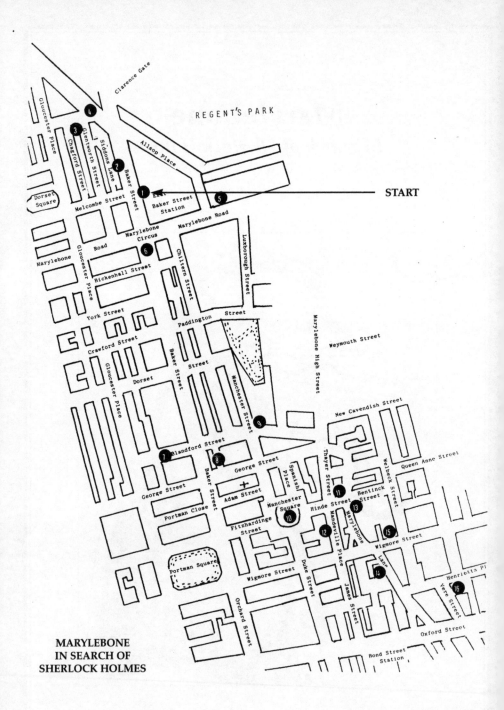

REGENT'S PARK

Clarence Gate

Gloucester Place

Chagford Street

Glentworth Street

Siddons Lane

Baker Street

Melcombe Street

Dorset Square

Allsop Place

START

Baker Street Station

Marylebone Circus

Marylebone Road

Luxborough Street

Marylebone Road

Gloucester Place

Marylebone

Bickenhall Street

Chiltern Street

Marylebone High Street

Weymouth Street

York Street

Paddington Street

Street

Crawford Street

Gloucester Place

Baker Street

Dorset

Street

New Cavendish Street

Manchester Street

Blandford Street

George Street

Spanish Place

Thayer Street

Welbeck Street

Queen Anne Street

George Street

Adam Street

Bentinck Street

Baker Street

Portman Close

Manchester Square

Hinde Street

Marylebone

Fitzhardinge Street

Mandeville Place

Wigmore Street

Portman Square

Wigmore Street

Duke Street

James Street

Lane

Henrietta Pl

Orchard Street

Bond Street Station

Oxford Street

Vere Street

**MARYLEBONE
IN SEARCH OF
SHERLOCK HOLMES**

Key to map

1.   Baker Street Underground Station

2.   Abbey National House

3.   St Cyprian's Parish Church

4.   Park Road

5.   London Planetarium and Madame Tussaud's

6.   Baker Street

7.   Blandford Street

8.   Kendall Place (Mews)

9.   Durrant's Hotel

10. Manchester Square

11. Hinde Street Methodist Church

12. Trinity College of Music

13. Bentinck Street

14. Marylebone Lane Police Station, site of

15. John Bell & Croyden - chemists

16. St Peter's Church, Vere Street

Marylebone

In search of Sherlock Holmes

Start: Baker Street Underground Station.

Circle, Bakerloo, Jubilee & Metropolitan Lines.

Connecting buses: 2A, 213, 13, 18, 27, 74, 82, 113, 139, 159, 274.

Time: allow approximately 3 hours.

Note: Not on the walk, but associated with and well worth a visit, is the Sherlock Holmes Public House at Northumberland Avenue out of Trafalgar Square. In the pub is a reconstruction of Holmes Study along with artifacts associated with the detective.

*T**he parish church of St Mary nestling by the Two (Ty) River. A "lost" village that has been absorbed into a great Metropolis - London. Many villages all over the countryside have tended to be founded either by a roadside or by the riverside. The ancient trade routes of bygone days when goods were sent by river or by track from place to place. Here is no exception. Marylebone is both by a river and a roadway viz, the River Tyburn, and the Oxford Road (Street). In the Middle Ages villages abounded beyond the immediate suburbs of the Cities of London and Westminster. The earliest mention of Marylebone can be found in the account of the area in the Doomsday Survey of 1086. At that time it was well known as either the Manor of Lilleston (the township of the Lilly family), or simply as Tyburn, as an area not just a river. It is not shown as St Mary Bourne until the 15th century, when the Tybourne Manor was owned by the Benedictine nuns of St Mary's Abbey, Barking. Prior to this time, the parish church was dedicated to St John and was located at the Oxford Road end of Marylebone Lane, then known as Lustie Lane. However, the church, being remote*

from the village, was under constant threat of vandals and, according to Newcourt's Repertorium, 1708, was robbed of its vestments, books, statues and bells in October 1400 when the Bishop of London, Robert Braybroke, 1381-1404, assented to the new church being erected near to the village where a small chapel-of-ease had already been established. It was hard by the river on land that was owned by John Lilleston, the then Lord of the Manor. To distinguish the new church from the former one, the dedication was changed from St John to St Mary. Saint Mary-le-bone was born! In the 16th century, Henry VIII, 1491 - 1547, acquired land in the north of the parish and turned it into a deerpark, the remains of which are now incorporated in Regent's Park. Until the early 18th century Mary-le-bone was still rural, thee village comprising of houses, shops, a tavern or two, and the parish church. With the opening of the Marylebone Pleasure Gardens, business and people were attracted to the area. The gardens rivalled Vauxhall and Ranelagh for musical concerts, scenic effects, illuminations and firework displays. The Manor could also boast the Lord Mayor (of London's) Banqueting House near the Oxford Road, and the gradual spread of the village to the City, and of the City's spread towards Marylebone.

With the greatly increased population and the spreading out of the houses it soon became evident that the one church was not sufficient for all the people living in the area. In 1724 a proprietary chapel, at first called the Marylebone Chapel and later the Oxford Chapel, was formally consecrated. The architect was James Gibbs, 1682 - 1754, who at the time of being commissioned to design the building was already working on his St Martin in the Fields church (see "A Walk with Charles Dickens")who decided to use his new project as a prototype. All the workmen connected with St Martin's were used for the new chapel which was to become a model for St Martin's. In the early 19th century an extensive restoration programme was carried out, and in 1832 the church was dedicated to St Peter. Evidence of the 18th century developments can still be seen in the lovely squares that abound in St Marylebone. Two later events have deeply influenced the area. First, in the 18th century the New Road was built, and second, in the 19th century the coming of the railways - both above and under the ground. Gone are the leafy lanes and the isolation that St Marylebone enjoyed in the past. It has become the hustle and bustle of the 20th century - motors and all! BUT for all that, there are still many places of interest, many lovely buildings to admire, and many stories to be told of this 'lost village' of London. We shall meet some of them on the walk.

Starting Point

(1) Baker Street Underground Station.

Opened in 1868 as part of the world's first underground railway systems - with Mr & Mrs Gladstone present at the official opening ceremony - the station is served by the Circle, Bakerloo, Metropolitan, and Jubilee Lines.

Leave the station by way of the Baker Street exit. Cross the road to the Abbey National Building Society's offices.

(2) Abbey National House

Today the House stands on numbers 217 to 223 Baker Street, which includes the number of the house in which Sherlock Holmes and Dr Watson resided. Only, at the time that Holmes "lived" in Baker Street, there was no 221 where there is today! The stretch of roadway from Marylebone Road to Park Road was listed as Upper Baker Street. This was continued southward by York Place, and then Baker Street itself. At the entrance to the building, there is a plaque commemorating Sherlock Holmes, while

if anybody writes, to him, and they still do, then they get a reply from Abbey National. For a person who did not exist in the flesh he certainly commands a devoted fan club. In 1974, in the New York Times, there appeared a letter from a distressed reader "It is shocking" the writer complained "to see your usually reliable paper publishing a reference to the late Sherlock Holmes, 'Late' indeed! Sherlock Holmes is alive and well. He has withdrawn from private practice, and is a trifle slow, but I can assure you Sherlock Holmes lives! Until the world's newspapers print his obituary, let all true believers take heart". It never fails to amaze people that a 'man' who existed only in the mind of a man, could attract and maintain such interest, such devotion by his 'fans'. The late Sir Conan Doyle, 1859 - 1930, was a medical graduate from Edinburgh University, and set up in practice at No 2 Devonshire Place. While he was waiting for patients he got bored. As a result, he "set pen to paper", and Sherlock Holmes was "born", and Conan Doyle had found an outlet for his talents.

After reading the inscription on the plaque, turn left, and walk down Baker Street to Melcombe Street. Turn right, past Siddons Lane, (a reminder that the famous 18th century actress lived in Upper Baker Street) to Glentworth Street. At the far end is…

(3) St Cyprian's Parish Church.

Built to the designs of the late Sir Ninian Comper, 1864 - 1960, the church was consecrated 1st June 1904, and represents a perfect example of a medieval style church erected in the 20th century. The outside is plain red brick, but once the visitor steps inside the building, it is like stepping back in time. The colours of the stained glass in the windows reflect handsomely on the wooden parquet flooring and on the stone of the steps around the altar. Across the entire width of the church there stretches the great Rood Screen, complete with painted figures of the saints of the Church.

It is hard to believe that the building was not built in the Middle Ages, and has escaped the ravages of the Reformation and Time itself. Vandalism, one of the great curses of the century, has meant that the church has to be kept locked unless the church-watchers are on duty. However, the church is used regularly for services during the week, and, of course, on Sunday there are the usual services of the Church of England.

Just beyond the church is Park Road, by way of Ivor Place.

(4)   Park Road, No. 23

Here lived Jose de San Martin, 1778 - 1850, the Argentine soldier and statesman. As a revolutionary he liberated Chile and Peru from Spanish occupation, the latter's independence was obtained by marching his army over the Andes, not by the more obvious route through Chile. He came to Europe, lived here for a time, but later left for France where he died in poverty in Boulogne.

Walk to the nearby road crossing and cross over Park Road to Allsop Place. At the end of the Place is Marylebone Road and...

(5)   The London Planetarium & Madame Tussaud's.

Madam Tussaud, 1761 - 1850, was employed by the Court of Louis XVI, 1754 - 1792, to make wax figures. At the height of the French

Revolution, 1789 - 1795, she was sent to prison, where she took models for the heads of victims of "Madam Guillotine". In 1802 she left France and settled in London bringing with her a grisly trunk of facsimiles of freshly chopped heads! Originally her waxworks were to be found in Baker Street, and then, in 1884 the family moved to the present site. In 1958 a planetarium was built to the side of the waxworks, and a combined ticket is available for both attractions.

Cross the Marylebone Road, and turn right walking towards Baker Street. Turn left into Baker Street.

(6)   Baker Street

Edward Baker of Runston in Dorset, was a speculative builder of the 18th century who gave his name to the street. Originally there were only 84 houses between Crawford Street and Portman Square. Later York Place and Upper Baker Street were joined together as Baker Street which nearly doubled the length, and gave it many more houses and shops.

Walk down Baker Street.

The Buildings and People of Baker Street

At No 15 Cardinal Wiseman 1802 - 1865, the first Post-Reformation Archbishop of Westminster, died. He was appointed Vicar Apostolic for the London District in 1847, and three years later raised to the dignity of Archbishop. Through his writings in the Dublin Review he was responsible for sowing doubts of the Catholicity of the Church of England in the the mind of the Revd. John Henry Newman, who, at that time, was the Vicar of the University church of St Mary in Oxford. Newman resigned from the living of St Mary's in 1843, and in 1845 entered the Roman Catholic Church, being elevated to the College of Cardinals in 1881.

On the opposite side of the roadway can be seen

a Post Office and next to it a building which has often been pointed out as being 'one of the homes of Sherlock Holmes and Dr Watson.

Post Offices played an important part in the life of the great detective, and it is easy to see how these two buildings have become linked with the stories of Conan Doyle's character.

There is, also in Baker Street, the Sherlock Holmes Hotel where meetings of the Sherlock Holmes Society take place who regularly hold dinners in his honour.

Further down Baker Street was the shop of Curtis the Chemist. A short distance from the residence of Holmes and Watson it is not hard to believe that Watson used the shop to obtain drugs for Holmes from here in an emergency.

At No 61, now the Head Office of the Marks and Spencer chain of shops stood, in Holmes's day, No 21 the original house of the great man himself. Conan Doyle, looking for a place to live in 1886 visited No 21 Baker Street, and turned it into 221B Baker Street. He further disguised the exact location reducing the number of windows on the front of the house. There is no evidence that he either bought the house or even lived in it himself. But he did install there Mrs Hudson, the housekeeper/owner of the house, who 'took in gentlemen lodgers', among whom were Holmes and Watson. In 1888, when Sherlock Holmes was 'born', in the case of the story of "A Study in Scarlet", he took up residence here. Now the mystery has been solved!

Continue down Baker Street until Blandford Street is reached. Turn left.

(7)   Blandford Street.

The street has no less than three houses all of which claim to have been lived in by Holmes at some time or other in his life. They are number 33, 21 and 19. On no 2 there is an original (Royal) Society of Arts plaque commemorating the working there of Michael Faraday 1791 - 1867. He was a bookseller's errand boy whose job it was to take papers to clients who had hired them to read. This task lasted for one year (1804) after which he secured an apprenticeship as a bookbinder. He was given an Encyclopedia to bind, and became deeply interested in an article about electricity and spent all his spare time pursuing his new found hobby. His interest led him to write to Sir Humphrey Davy, 1778 - 1829, the English chemist who studied the effects of electric currents on compounds, who secured for himself a position of assistant in the laboratory of the Royal Institution in Abermarle Street, off Piccadilly, where there is a small museum devoted to his work today.

On the right hand side of the street is Kendal Place, formerly Kendal Mews.

(8)   Kendal Place (Mews).

The Mews (Place) run parallel to Baker Street and include the rear of No 34 from which the mysterious marksman tried to shoot Holmes while he was sitting in his study at No 221B Baker Street. Thanks to the help that Holmes received from Madam Tussaud's Waxworks a dummy head was placed in the window and he went unharmed. A reconstruction of the study, complete with wax head, can be seen at the Sherlock Holmes public house in Northumberland Avenue, just off Trafalgar Square.

Walk along to the junction of Blandford Street and Manchester Street. Here can be seen...

(9)   Durrant's Hotel.

Here Sherlock Holmes would meet clients who for some reason or other did not wish to be seen entering his residence in Baker Street. The hotel has been described as being the "poor man's Brown's Hotel" where afternoon tea was served but not with the grandeur of "the other place". Do Holmes's clients wait for him here?

Turn right and walk down Manchester Street, noting on the way the delightful Coade stone key-stones of some of the houses.

Coade Stone

Coade stone was manufactured on the site where the Royal Festival Hall now stands on South Bank. It was an artificial stone made by the Coade Family from a formula which remains unknown today. Also, look out for the 'blue-plaque' commemorating Sir Francis Beaufort, 1774 - 1857, admiral and hydrographer, on No 51 where he lived.

At the end of Manchester Street is...

(10) Manchester Square.

The square was laid out between 1776 and 1788, and is dominated on the north side by Hertford House, now housing the Wallace Collection. George Montagu, the fourth Duke of Manchester, built the house in the 18th century, and the square followed later. The Collection is particularly rich in paintings, furniture and porcelain of 18th century France, with a fine additional collection of European arms and armour, and was mainly formed by the Fourth Marquees of Hertford, Richard Seymour-Conway, 1800 - 1870. Included in the collection is a painting by Claude Joseph Vernet, 1714 - 1789, who appears in the story of the "Greek Interpreter". It shows him to be Sherlock Holmes's grandmother's brother on his mother's side!!

There was another member of the same family who played a part in the life story of Holmes and Watson, it was a certain Doctor Vernet or Verner (the English form of the name). He appears in the story of the "Norwood Builder", which appeared originally in the Strand Magazine for November 1903. It was Doctor Verner who bought Doctor Watson's medical practice in Kensington in order that he (Watson) might devote more time with Holmes. Watson was said to be furious when he later

discovered that Verner was "a distant relation of Holmes", and that Holmes himself had put up the money for the transaction. Today, the square is still a pleasant oasis of 18th century charm and elegance, except the corner nearest to the Wallace Collection which has been rebuilt in a modern style not in keeping with the rest of the square.

Walk round the square, noting the following houses where persons of note have lived and which are marked by 'blue-plaques'.

No 14 here lived Lord Milner, 1854 - 1925, the statesman, who held a number of government offices during his long and successful career.

No 3 was home to J H Jackson, 1835 - 1911, the physician who was an expert on diseases of the nervous system for forty years.

No 2 the composer of "The Lilley of Killarney", Sir Julius Benedict, 1804 - 1885, and many other popular operas who spent the last forty years of his life here.

Leave the square by way of Hinde Street where can be found...

(11) Hinde Street Methodist Church.

Built in 1881 - 1887 to the designs of the architect Weir, the church is the University Chaplaincy for Methodists in London. Its two-storied portico was described by the late Professor Sir Nikolaus Pevsner, in his "Buildings of England - London", as being "à la St Paul's Cathedral". The street is named after a tenant farmer, Jacob Hinde, who leased part of Marylebone Park (now Regent's Park) from 1765 to 1803. Herbert Spencer, 1820 - 1903, the philosopher, lived at No 6 from 1862 to 1863, and was, together with Thomas Huxley, 1825 - 1895, the biologist, an ardent supporter of Charles Darwin, 1809 - 1882, the philosophic scientist. Rose Macaulay, 1881 - 1958, the author, lived at No 20, from 1941 to her death. She wrote her first novel, "The

Valley of the captives", published in 1911 when she was still studying at Oxford University. Her epigrammatic style endeared her to her readers, in 1956 she won the James Tait Black.Memorial Prize for her last novel, "The Tower of Trebizond". The Prize is one of the oldest still extant in the publishing world, having been instituted in 1918 in memory of a partner of A and C Black Ltd.

On the corner of Hinde Street and Mandeville Place stands...

(12) Trinity College of Music.

Founded in 1872 as the School for the study and practice of Music for the Church, it has grown to become the second most important musical college in London. The two former buildings, Nos 11 and 13 Mandeville Place, were joined together in 1922, and the portico and entrance to the College built. Over the porch can be seen the coat of arms of the college with its motto "Gloria in excelsis deo".

Return to Hinde Street and walk along to the corner of...

(13) Bentinck Street.

The grandson of Hans Bentinck, the 'arranger' of the marriage of William III, 1650 - 1702, to Mary II, 1662 - 1694, William Bentinck married into the Earl of Harley family, and so acquired land in the area. In more recent years the street was home to Guy Burgess and Anthony Blunt in the 1940s. It was while about to cross from Hinde Street into Marylebone Lane that Holmes was nearly run over by a speeding van. "My dear Watson Professor Moriarty is not a man to let the grass grow under his feet. I went out about mid-day to transact some business in Oxford Street. As I passed the corner which leads from Bentinck Street ... a two-horsed van, furiously driven, whizzed by and was on me like a flash. I sprang for the foot-path and saved myself by the fraction of a second. The van dashed round into

Marylebone Lane and was gone". The story is told in the "Final Problem", which appeared originally in the Strand and McClure's Magazine in December 1893.

Turn right down Marylebone Lane, which follows the route of the River Tyburn at this point to Wigmore Street. The Lane continues across the Street.

(14) Marylebone Lane Police Station.

Here was the local police station for Baker Street, and was 'closely associated' with Holmes and his investigations from time to time. During the 1880s there was an Inspector Holmes in the "A" division of the Metropolitan Police, and an Inspector James Sherlock, as well as a Chief Inspector William Sherlock, both of "B" division. It all adds up!

Return to Wigmore Street and turn right,. noting on the way...

(15) John Bell & Croyden the chemist.

Its former 24 hour service was undoubtedly used by both Holmes and Watson for whom Wigmore Street was a popular shopping place. Here Holmes could, and did, obtain cocaine legally in the 19th century. Today, it is a Schedule 4 drug and is only available on prescription. Holmes was a drug addict, and would, obviously not have wished to be seen buying the drug, either in quantity or regularly, from the local chemist shop in Baker Street (Curtis shop we have already noted). Other people have also used the shop for drugs, notably Mrs Meybrick and Madeline Smith both of whom purchased poison here for murderous purposes. Holmes would almost certainly have died from cocaine had not Doctor Watson taken him in hand.

Wigmore Street is mentioned in the "Sign of Four" when Holmes sends Watson to a Post Office and he returns to Baker Street with dust on his shoes. Holmes deduces which office he had been to by the dust on his shoes. The pair also passed through the street on their way to the Alpha Inn in "Blue Carbuncle", which appeared originally in the Strand Magazine in January 1892. It concerned James Ryder, the upper attendant at the Hotel Cosmopolitan, who stole the Countess of Morcar's jewel.

Walk along Wigmore Street to Welbeck Street. Turn right and walk to Vere Street. Here is to be found...

(16) St Peter's Church, Vere Street.

With the development of the Earl of Oxford's estate in the 18th century the needs arose for the building of a place of worship for those families living here. Commissioned by Edward Harley, Earl of Oxford in the 1720s, it was designed by James Gibbs, 1682 - 1754, and consecrated on Easter Day 1727. Originally called the Marylebone Chapel, and later the Oxford Chapel, it did not acquire parochial status until 1832, when it was dedicated to St Peter. Prior to the 19th century it was a Proprietary Chapel, that is a Church of

England chapel built by subscription and maintained by private individuals. The ministers of these chapels were normally granted a bishop's licence to minister, but only with the full consent of the vicar of the parish. There are still one or two such chapels left in London today, most having been either given parochial status or demolished. St Peter's is considered to have been the proto-type for the architect's pièce-de-rèsistance, St Martin in the Fields, by Trafalgar Square.

A brick nearly struck Holmes while he was walking here one day. In "The Final Problem", he records "I walked down Vere Street, a brick came down from the roof of one of the buildings and shattered in fragments at my feet. I called the police and had the place examined. There were bricks and slates piled on the roof prior to repairs and they would have me believe that they had toppled over. Of course, I know better..."

From the church it is a short walk down Vere Street to Oxford Street, with a choice of Oxford Circus, or Bond Street underground stations.

Pimlico and
Belgravia
Passport to Another World

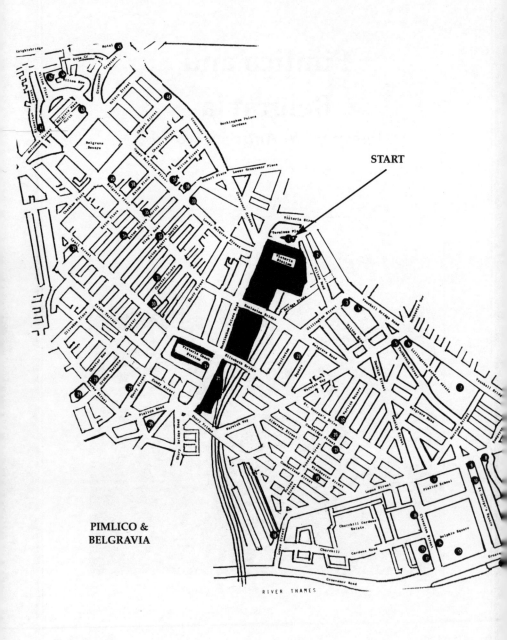

START

PIMLICO &
BELGRAVIA

RIVER THAMES

Key to map

1. Terminus Place
2. Apollo Victoria Theatre
3. Joseph Conrad "blue-plaque"
4. Queen Mother Sports Centre
5. Tachbrook Street Market
6. Lillingstone Estate
7. Parish Church of St James the Less
8. The Gallery Public House
9. Parish Church of St Saviour's
10. St George's Square
11. Pimlico School
12. Pimlico Gardens
13. Dolphin Square
14. Claverton Street (right-hand side)
15. Claverton Street (left-hand side)
16. Methodist Church, site of
17. Whitely House, Churchill Gardens Estate
18. Peabody Avenue
19. Holy Apostles (Catholic) Church
20. Parish Church of St Gabriel
21. Aubrey Beardsley's House
22. Warwick Square
23. Eccleston Square
24. Victoria Coach Station
25. National Audit Office
26. Parish Church of St Barnabas
27. 180 Ebury Street (Mozart Plaque)
28. Parish Church of St Mary Bourne Street
29. Grey Coat Hospital, Lower School
30. Parish Church of St Michael Chester Square
31. 24 Chester Square (Mary Shelley, nee Godwin)
32. Eaton Square
33. Eaton Square Nos 1 - 4 (Lord Boothby)
34. Eaton Square No 80 (George Peabody)
35. Belgium Embassy
36. Parish Church of St Peter, Eaton Square
37. Walter Bagehot ("blue-plaque")
38. John Lubbock ("blue-plaque")
39. Thomas Cubitt ("blue-plaque")
40. Lord John Russell ("blue-plaque")
41. Norwegian Embassy
42. Turks Head Public House
43. Parish Church of St Paul Knightsbridge
44. Alfonso Lopez-Pumarejo ("blue-plaque")
45. Grenadier Public House
46. Grosvenor Gardens Mews
47. Lanesborough Hotel
48. Grosvenor Place

Pimlico and Belgravia

Passport to Another World

Start: Victoria Underground Station.

Circle, District and Victoria Lines.

Connecting buses: 2, 2A, 2B, 8, 11, 16, 24, 36, 36B, 52, 73, 82, 177EX, 185, 239, 507, 511, C1, C10.

Time: allow approximately 3 hours.

The walk can be divided into two, visiting Pimlico and Belgravia separately. In each case the separate walks start and finish at Victoria Underground Station. To start the first walk start as though you are doing the whole walk from 1 - 2 etc. To start the second walk or half way through the complete walk from Terminus place, turn left up Buckingham Palace Road towards Victoria Coach Station **(24)** from where you start.

*U*p to the early nineteenth century the area covered by this walk was, more or less, still open countryside - with just a house or two along the roadside south of Hyde Park. Among the exceptions was the house that had been built in 1719 for James Lane, 2nd Viscout Lanesborough. It was here in 1733 that the St George's Hospital was founded by a group of disgruntled governors of the Westminster Hospital. The cause of their disagreement was based on the lack of room given in the hospital for charitable purposes. Here they were able to offer "the poor and needy" not only the medical attention that they needed, but also a place where they would benefit from the country air "which in the general opinion of the physicians would be more effectual than physic in the cure of many distempers such as may affect the poor, who live in close and confined spaces within these great cities".

An Act of Parliament of 1826 allowed Lord Grosvenor, the land owner to "drain the site and raise the level". So began the extending of the western boundary of the Cities of London and Westminster, and the creating of the largest of the Duke of Westminster's London Estates - Belgravia and Pimlico.

Today this estate stretches from Knightsbridge in the north to the Grosvenor Road in the south.

Most of the street names, etc, reflect the places and titles held by the Dukes of Westminster since the family were created baronets in the seventeenth century. Their dukedom dates from 1874.

Authorities differ over whether or not the present day Belgravia and Pimlico were once known simply as Pimlico. However, George V always contended that his correct address was H M King George V, Buckingham Palace, Pimlico, London SW1. Some maps have also shown the Wellington Arch at the end of Constitution Hill as "The Pimlico Arch". John Rocque' map of 1737 shows the roadway by the wall of Buckingham Palace's gardens simply as "Pimlico".

The walk has been devised as one walk with the option of being used as two separate walks. This has been made possible by covering Pimlico and Belgravia by starting and ending at Victoria Station.

BELGRAVIA is a sobriquet originally being applied to Belgrave and Eaton Squares.

PIMLICO was probably copied from a pleasure garden in Hoxton that took its name from the sixteenth century proprietor, Pimlico itself being home to one or two gardens. An alternative derivation comes from the Pimlico tribe of Red Indians who exported timber to England in the seventeenth century. A timber yard and Timber Wharf are clearly marked on the Ordnance Survey of the area of 1894.

Starting Point

(1) Terminus Place - Victoria Station.

Terminus Place is sandwiched between the underground railway station, the 'bus station and the British Rail station at Victoria. To the side of the railway station is Wilton Road, with immediately on the left hand side of the roadway the Apollo Victoria Theatre (2).

(2) The Apollo Victoria Theatre.

Built in 1929 to the designs of E Alsmsley Lewis as the New Victoria Theatre and has since been renamed the Apollo Victoria. When it first opened the building was among the earliest buildings to use the Continental style of bands horizontally across the outside with windows of a similar pattern. Its interior retains the elaborate decoration that was freely used in the late 1920s and 1930s.

Walk down Wilton Road until Gillingham Street. Cross over the road and turn left walking towards Vauxhall Bridge Road. On the right hand side look out for…

(3) 17 Gillingham Street.

On No 17 is a "blue-plaque" commemorating Joseph Conrad the Polish born English novelist whose writings are said to be a combination of stirring adventures coupled with human psychology.

At the end of the street turn right into Vauxhall Bridge Road. The road was part of the development plan for the area in the early nineteenth century. Laid out in 1816 there are few of the later houses that lined the roadway left "in situ" today. Much further development has taken place in more recent years. Shortly on the right hand side is…

(4) The Queen Mother Sports Centre.

Opened by Her Majesty Queen Elizabeth the Queen Mother in 1980, it offers a wide range of sporting activities to its clients.

From the Centre a short walk brings the explorer to Tachbrook Street on the right. Turn into Tachbrook Street.

(5) Tachbrook Street.

The street is built on land which a royal gardener of the eighteenth century, Henry Wise, purchased in 1713, and who, on his retirement, became a country gentleman in Warwickshire. He owned estates at Moreton and Lillingston as well as Charlwood, in Surrey. When his land in Pimlico was acquired by the Duke of Westminster it was decided to commemorate the previous owner. There is also a Henry Wise House on the Lillingston Estate in the Vauxhall Bridge Road. At the junction of the street with Warwick Way there is a very pleasant week-day market. Thanks to the Westminster City Council's pedestrianising of the area it has become a "safe area" for the young and old. In the main the stalls sell foodstuffs, but on Saturdays there can usually be found other stalls to entice the week-end shopper to buy "something extra".

Extending down the entire length on the left hand side of the road is Lillingston Estate designed by Darbourne and Dark and completed in 1973 with Longmore Gardens being added in 1980. A walk through the estate will show the walker how it is possible to create a new, friendly, environment on a site that had previously been closely knitted together with nineteenth century housing. Care should be taken however not to make a noise or in any way disturb the relaxing atmosphere of the area.

At Moreton Street turn left and walk along to…

(6) The Parish Church of St James' the Less

The church was built in memory of James Henry Monk, Bishop of Gloucester, 1830 - 1856 by George Edmund Street, on behalf of the bishop's three sisters - "The Miss Monks". It was Street's first church in London and, when it was first completed caused a great deal of criticism from the architectural critics of the day. Being built of bricks, black and red, and "looking foreign" and rising... "as a lily among weeds" as the "Illustrated London News" says in its review of the church building - it has mellowed with the intervening years and the style has become an accepted one of the nineteenth century Like so many churches in London, and elsewhere, it is normally locked against vandals and thieves. Times of the Sunday services are on the noticeboard. The parish hall and school are now used for other purposes. Around the buildings can be seen a very fine range of wrought-iron railings.

Return to Tachbrook Street and continue straight on. At the end of Tachbrook Street is Lupus Street. Cross the road and turn right. On the left hand side of the road and at the junction of Aylesford Street is...

(7) "The Gallery Public House".

A nineteenth century house with outside seating for the fine weather, and a pleasant inside with prints on the walls.

Aylesford Street leads to the Tachbrook Estate. At the head of St George's Square (10) is...

(9) The Parish Church of St Saviour's.

Described by Basil Clarke in his "Parish Churches of London", as being "another Middle-Pointed church by Thomas Cundy of Kentish rag". Consecrated in July 1864 costing £12,000, it had further improvements made to the interior in 1882 when a faculty (diocesan permission) was granted to carve the capitals of the pillars, the corbels of the roof and to erect a reredos behind the high altar. At the same time the galleries around the church were also removed. Prior to the First World War, 1914 - 1918, a vestry was added to the north side of the church by Nicholson and Corlette. Most of the stained glass of the windows is by Clayton and Bell.

Opposite the west end of the church is...

(11) The Pimlico School.

Loved by a few and hated by a few more, the school was designed by the Greater London Council's architect John Bancroft between 1966 and 1970. It houses nearly two thousand children and was once described as being "the weirdest building to appear in London to date". It lies in a man made depression and makes a very striking contrast to all the buildings that surround it.

Walk down the side of St George's Square on the right hand side with its 1840s houses. At the end of the square cross over the roadway (Grosvenor Road) to...

(12) Pimlico Gardens.

The gardens provide a pleasant break in walking the streets of Pimlico and a chance to watch the various activities of the River Thames on whose banks the gardens are to be found. The statue is that of William Husskisson, the statesman whose claim to fame but not of fortune, lies in the fact that he was the first fatal accident of the railway system. He attended the opening of the Liverpool and Manchester Railway in 1830 and while re-entering the train after a water stop for the engine was crushed to death by another passing train. I wonder if we would have ever heard of him if he hadn't. On the opposite side of the gardens to the statue is the Westminster Boating Base for all those who "like messing about in boats".

On leaving the gardens turn left and shortly on the opposite side of the road can be seen...

(13) Dolphin Square.

Built in 1937 to the designs of Gordon Jeeves with 1236 flats arranged around a central garden and occupying 7.6 acres (3.1 ha). Within the complex there is a public restaurant, a sports centre and an underground car park with a capacity for two hundred cars. The residents in recent years have varied from thespians to spies, from professional ladies and gentlemen to politicians and their wives. The square takes its name from the dolphin (water pump) that drew water from the river near here. It was built on a former army clothing depot.

Cross the road to Claverton Street (14), named after one of the villages on the Grosvenor Estates in Cheshire.

(14) Claverton Street.

The street today presents the nineteenth century houses on the right hand side, and the twentieth century housing estate (15) on the other. Opposite Chichester Street in the nineteenth century stood the Methodist Chapel that was attended by Mr and Mrs Bartlett (16). Adelaide Bartlett fell in love with the Chapel's minister, the outcome of which led to her being tried for the murder of her husband. Because the evidence was only circumstantial she was acquitted, after which she disappeared. Their home was number 85 on which now stands (17) Whitely House of the Churchill Gardens Estate.

To wander through Churchill Gardens Estate, by way of Churchill Gardens Road, is to "enter another world". A world of concrete slabs with greenery and sun between them. The architects, Powell and Moya, were still at the Architectural Association at the time they won the competition for this, then, "totally new form of urban life". Hallfield Estate in Paddington, another shining light of Post-Second World War housing scene did not appear until the 1950s. Originally the Gardens' tenants received their hot water from the surplus of the Battersea Power Station across the river. When that building was closed down the Westminster City Council installed the estates own supply. Within the area of the estate only two former buildings were allowed to stay. One was the local church school - St Gabriel's Church of England Primary - built in the nineteenth century, with later additions. The other was the Parish House and halls and although agitated for during the last decade of the nineteenth century, it was not finally built until early in the twentieth century. The Revd. T F Shirley records in his book, "The first hundred years" "...the opening ceremony took place on 6 June 1901... a procession which left the church including the vicar, assistant clergy, the Bishop of London, and the band of the Church Lads' Brigade... the first meeting... St George's Slate Club on 20 June...".

At the end of Churchill Gardens Road turn right. Passing on the opposite side of the road...

(18) Peabody Avenue.

The Avenue is one of a number of Peabody Estates built, in the nineteenth century, through the benevolence of Mr George Peabody an American philanthropist. After he had amassed a large fortune when dealing in the foreign exchange and US securities in his native country, spent most of it on charitable institutions. Later, in 1862, he set about helping to solve the problem of inexpensive housing for the poor. His Trust Fund enabled the construction of houses for the workers. Ironically, the places where the Trust bought land in the nineteenth century were considered either "out of the way". or, "unsuitable for housing". Today these sites are within some of the richest locations in the Capital viz. Pimlico, Chelsea and the area just north of The Strand.

Walk along Lupus Street, so called after Hugh Lupus Grosvenor the son of the 3rd Marquis and later the 1st Duke of Westminster. Cross the roadway and turn into Winchester Street. Here is to be seen...

(19) The Roman Catholic Church of the Holy Apostles.

The church is the replacement Catholic Church for one that was bombed in April 1941. The original church had been housed in what had been the Wesleyan Chapel in Claverton Street, whose presence we have already noted. The church was consecrated by Cardinal Godfrey, Cardinal Archbishop of Westminster, on 9th November 1957. The site had been houses before the War but had been badly damaged in the Blitz of 1940 - 1941 and the then Parish Priest, Father Hadfield, purchased the site in 1948 from Cubitt's Estates for the sum of £7,000. Due to the building priorities of the time, housing and commerce taking preference over all other forms of buildings, the parish had to wait until 1955 before permission could be given to commence the work. The site had been well chosen and is well used. In addition to the church, there is a substantial hall underneath and, with access from Cumberland Street, the Priests' House joins on to the church building. To many residents and visitors alike the church itself presents a cool in summer, warm in winter, place in which to take a well earned rest, or the chance to have a quiet word with God.

On leaving the church turn left and walk to Sussex Street with its shops and flats offering a welcome to the passer-by. A short way along can be seen the entrance to the Westminster Play Association's playspace for children, constructed at basement level of houses destroyed in the last War and not rebuilt. Here local children can safely play under supervision of play-leaders.

After crossing Cambridge Street the walker arrives at...

(20) The Parish Church of St Gabriel, Warwick Square.

Built in 1853 to the designs of Thomas Cundy, Junior, it stands proud at the western side of the square. Its five aisles present the visitor who enters the church through the north west tower doorway, with a vast expanse of the nave and the two side aisles either side. Looking towards the east the eye of the visitor alights on the great High Altar designed by John Bentley, the architect of Westminster Cathedral, and the superb alabaster decoration around the sanctuary. Following the High Church tradition, there is often the smell of incense and the two shrines, one to St Gabriel and the other to the Blessed Virgin Mary, have votive candles standing in front of them. Like many other churches, St Gabriel's is seldom open to members of the public other than at the times of the services. Opposite the church's west porch at No 114 (21) Cambridge Street is the "blue-plaque" commemorating Aubrey Beardsley, artist who lived here from 1893 to 1895. He was regarded by many as being the "most talented artist of the 'decadent' school of the nineties", the first commission that earned any money was Malory's "Morte d'Arthur" from J M Dent, the publishers. Previously he had lived at No 32, at the time when he was still employed as an insurance clerk in the City. There is no plaque on this particular house.

Another house in the same street, No 21, without a plaque, was lived in by Mary Ann Evans, alias George Eliot, the nineteenth century novelist. She left the house when she went to live with George Lewis - before she married him.

(22) Warwick Square.

The Square was laid out in 1843 and still contains many fine houses from that time. Alas, today most of them are divided into flats such is the way of the world. The gardens in the centre of the square are "Private" and are maintained as such by the Warwick Gardens Committee whose members and subscribers all live in the immediate area of the square itself.

Before the development of this area, in the 1830s and 1840s, much of the land was below the high tide level of the river. The land was cultivated by professional gardeners who, on hearing of the proposals for its future, promptly planted expensive and exotic plants thereby raising the value of their land. Before the various streets and squares could be laid out and built on, thousands of tons of earth had to be moved here. Fortunately for the property owners, new and large docks were being build, east of London, and they were able to purchase large amounts of soil that was surplus to requirements by the docks.

At the end of the square turn left into Belgrave Road and walk towards Eccleston Square **(23)**.

(23) Eccleston Square.

The square was laid out in 1835 and, like its neighbours, consists largely of houses that have either been converted into flats or used as offices. In the centre is one of the best kept squares in London, which is open to members of the general public several times a year when the entrance fees are all donated to charity.

At No 34 there is an unofficial "blue-plaque" recording that Winston Spencer Churchill lived here between 1909 and 1913. It was while living here that he, as Home Secretary in the Liberal Government, became involved in the infamous "Sidney Street (Whitechapel) Siege". In January 1911, troops and armed police were used to evict from the Whitechapel house a group of anarchists led by "Peter the Painter". All the national newspapers carried photographs of Winston Churchill at the scene.

From the house, walk to Elizabeth Bridge, and turn right to soon reach Buckingham Palace Road. On the opposite side of the road can be seen...

(24) Victoria Coach Station.

Built in 1931 - 32 to the designs of WIllis

Gilbert and Partners demonstrating the modernistic style of the 1930s. Described as being "London's only modern transport terminal", it has won a place in the hearts of Londoners, and others, who use its facilities by the thousands every year. There have been, abortive, attempts to re-site the coach station elsewhere in the Capital but all have failed.

If you wish to divide the walk into two, turn right along Buckingham Palace Road to Terminus Place. To continue, turn left and continue to walk along Buckingham Palace Road to soon reach...

(25) The National Audit Office.

The offices were built in 1939 by A Lakenham as the British Airways Terminal, BA being the successor to Imperial Airways. In 1958 - 1960 an extension to the building was added.

Further on at Ebury Bridge cross over Buckingham Palace Road to Pimlico Road. A short distance along on the right hand side can be seen Coleshill House, another of the Peabody Estate housing projects, that is "well-kept and well-positioned" for its residents. On the corner of St Barnabas Street stands the Church of England Primary School for the parish. Next to it is...

(26) The Parish Church of St Barnabas, Pimlico.

Another of the Thomas Cundy churches, for the "new" estate of Pimlico in the early part of the nineteenth century. Work began in 1847 and the church was ready for worship five years later - to the day 11th June. The style is Early English (thirteenth century) in inspiration, using nineteenth century building techniques. As in many churches built in the last century, they come "complete" with vicarage and church school altogether on the same site. Originally it was a "breakaway church" from St Paul's Knightsbridge. While the Ecclesiologist gave its seal of approval to the building, others, notably the anti-papists of the time, did not approve of the "goings-on" in the church. It was in 1850 that the Pep Pius IX, re-established the Roman Hierarchy in England bringing fresh cries of "No-Popery" in the streets of London. Such cries had not been heard so vehemently since Lord George Gordon had led similar attacks in the previous century. This did not stop the parish from continuing its ritualistic practices! Later additions to the church's ornaments include a reredos by Bodley and Garner in 1893, a Lady Chapel in 1900 by Ninian Comper, a baptistery by Fredk. Hunt 1901, and in 1953 Comper designed the glass in the great East Window.

Return to Pimlico Road cross over the roadway and walk to...

(27) Ebury Street.

At no 180 the young Wolfgang Amadeus Mozart lodged with his parents in 1764 and composed his first symphony here. At that time, the address was Fivefields Row, Chelsea, the name reflecting the Five Fields which made up the area until the development of the estate in the nineteenth century. Ebury Street, takes its name from the title given to the area at the time of the Domesday book (1086) that of EIA, meaning 'well-watered'. This developed into Eiabury (bury being a Saxon word for 'house"); therefore a house built on the eia, and

eventually becoming Ebury of today. The street has been home to many famous persons over the years including Noel Coward, who lived at No 111 in the 1920s.

At the junction of Ebury Street and Pimlico Road is Bourne Street. Walk along the street and just past Graham Terrace is the Parish Church of St Mary (28).

(28) The Church of St Mary.

Built between 1873 and 1874 as a chapel of ease to St Barnabas but later in 1909 granted parochial status, it was designed by R J Withers. The architect had the reputation of building "a good cheap type of brick church", this was one of them. It cost £4,500 and is a good example both of his work and of the type of town churches that the nineteenth century produced by the dozen all over London. An extension to the building was added in 1927 by H S Goodhart-Rendell. The High Altar, the work of S Gambier Parry, was re-modelled by Martin Travers c1919. The overall atmosphere is Baroque, considered by some members of the Church of England as being the "brand make" of Anglo-Catholicism. There are 'smells and bells' at all the right places, and the music is "out-of-this-world"!

On the opposite side of the road is (29) the Lower School of the Grey Coat Hospital whose Upper School and original site is in Grey Coat Place "just behind Victoria Street and close to the Army and Navy Stores there!"

Return to Graham Terrace recalling William Graham who, in the early nineteenth century leased some land here from the Grosvenor Family. Shortly afterwards he developed the land into housing. It is a still "back-water" to wander along and to wonder as to whom lived in these comparative small houses in the 1820s.

At the end of the terrace is Eaton Terrace,

turn left and walk along to Chester Row. Turn right along Chester Row, cross Elizabeth Street and continue to Chester Square. Here is...

(30) The Parish Church of St Michael's Chester Square.

Built in 1846, to the designs of Thomas Cundy and is considered to be typical of his Pimlico/Belgravia churches of the time. Here he chose the Decorated Style (fourteenth century) architecture. The foundation stone was laid 20th May 1844 by the Marquis of Westminster. He was one of the most generous parishioners in his contributions towards the building costs. Two years later the church was consecrated. A faculty dated February 1910 gave the vicar, churchwardens and parishioners permission to erect a reredos of alabaster, decorate the chancel walls, pave the chancel with marble and renew the holy table (altar). This they did, and so matters stayed until the 1920s when Giles Scott was called in to add a Memorial Chapel, and a new reredos replaced the one previously mentioned. Noteworthy stained glass is in the two windows by William Morris (1882) and the west window designed by Hugh Easton in 1951. Today the church is a great centre for maintaining the Protestant Faith held so deeply by one section of the Church of England.

Walk around the square starting on the north side where can be seen...

(31) The Houses of Chester Square.

No 24 the home of Mary Godwin who became Percy Shelley's second wife. It was the home of Shelley's mother and the engraved stone beneath the ground floor window gives the house as the place of Mary Shelley's death in 1851. No 14 was the home of Harold Macmillan in the 1920s (there is no plaque recording the fact - yet). No 8, after the death of her husband, Mrs Neville Chamberlain lived

and died here (1967). There is a plaque at No 77 that shows that Queen Wilhehmina of the Netherlands had her Secretariat here during the Second World War, after which she returned to Holland where she abdicated in 1948 and was succeeded by her only child Queen Juliana. At the far end of the square from the church are Nos 1 and 2. No 2 was the home of Matthew Arnold for ten years in the nineteenth century, and, next door, No 1 was the home of Ralph Richardson, the thespian, in the 1950s.

Leave Chester Square for Lower Belgrave Street. Turn left and walk along to...

(32) Eaton Square.

The square was first laid out in 1828, but the building of the houses around it lasted only until 1855. The architect responsible for the square was Thomas Cubitt. Strictly speaking the shape of the area is a very elongated oblong with a main road (King's Road) dividing the two longest sides (North Side and South Side). Wandering along the two sides it is possible to notice the differing dates of the buildings. Yet they all seem to make up rows of terraced houses. To read the Parliamentary Electoral Roll is like reading a page out of "Who's Who", or "Debrett's Peerage". At Nos 1 - 4 lived Robert, Lord Boothby, politician, author and broadcaster from 1946 to 1986 **(33).**

Cross over to No 8 to walk down the south side of the square.

No 12 was the home of Osbert Lancaster the cartoonist, satirist and theatrical designer. His best known, and loved, character was Maudie Littlehampton in the Daily Express. No 17 in the 1870s was the residence of General William

Knollys who retired from active military duties and became the Controller and Treasurer to the Prince of Wales (later Edward VII). In the next block lived Neville Chamberlain in the 1930s before becoming Prime Minister in 1937 and moving to No 10 Downing Street. Seven doors away at No 44, Prince Matternich, the Austrian Statesman lived who presided over the Congress of Vienna. He was finally driven away to go and live in Brighton by the incessant piano playing of his neighbours (the Minto Family) daughters.

The square continues to the end of the terrace where it meets South Eaton Place, turn right, noting on the left hand side of the roadway two detached porches belonging to Nos 66 and 66A Eaton Square. Cross over King's Road and walk along the north side of the square. Here can be seen...

(34) The House of George Peabody.

No 80 the home of George Peabody and where he died in 1869. At first he was buried in Westminster Abbey, a rare honour for one not born in the United Kingdom. Shortly afterwards his body was removed and taken to Danvers in the United States and reburied. The town in Massachusetts was then renamed Peabody. At the junction of Eaton Square and Lyall Street is the Belgium Embassy (35) on whose wall can be seen a plaque commemorating Belgians who volunteered their services during the Second World War. The plaque was unveiled by H M Queen Elizabeth the Queen Mother in 1964. No 90 was the home of W S Gilbert, of Gilbert and Sullivan operettas fame. Gilbert lived here after the death of Sullivan in 1900. Although he tried to repeat the successful partnership by working with Edward German, their attempts to do so failed. The charisma between G & S could not be repeated. the last of the plaques of the square in on No 93 and recalls that it had been the home of Stanley Baldwin, who, somewhat unexpectedly, succeeded Bonar Law

as Prime Minister. During his time of office he had to contend with the General Strike of 1926 and the abdication of Edward VIII in 1937, after which he resigned and was given an earldom. When he died he was buried in Worcester Cathedral.

At the end of the square is. . .

(36) The Parish Church of St Peter.

The full and somewhat complicated beginnings of this church are carefully recorded in the vestry minutes of the "mother parish" - viz St George's, Hanover Square. Sufficient to record here that the present structure of the building was the final choice of the Church Commissioners who made a contribution towards its costs of £5,556 of the sum required (£22,427). During the late nineteenth century, the church was crowded for all its services in

spite of being able to seat 1,650 persons many others brought camp-stools to sit on while others had to stand. In 1873 a chancel was added by Blomfeld who also altered the layout *of the interior. The church continued to flourish and then, on 10th October 1987, disaster struck the church building was gutted by fire - the work of an arsonist. Four years later, to the day the restored interior was opened to the public once more. The new work was carried out by John and Nikki Braithwaite - parishioners and architects. "It is a building designed to be the focus of the local community for the 21st century" (so reads the brochure at the back of the church).*

On leaving the church turn right and walk along upper Belgrave Street. Here, on the Wilton Street side of the street can be seen…

(37) Plaque to Walter Bagehot.

The "blue-plaque" to Walter Bagehot, economist, banker and writer, who after his father-in-law's death (he married the daughter of Sir James Wilson, the founder and owner of the "Economist") took over the editorship of the "Economist".

Carry on along Upper Belgrave Street to Eaton Place. Turn left. Here lived at…

No 5 Lord Carson, the Solicitor-General, at the turn of the century and, although born in Dublin, opposed the plan for Home Rule in Ireland. No 16 proudly displays the plaque to William Ewart, politician and reformer. He was one of the originators of the erection of plaques on buildings of architectural and historical interest. On the opposite side of Eaton Place at No 29 **(38)** the home of John Lubbock, later Lord Avebury, is commemorated. He was born here and spent the first six years of his life in this house. His father, a banker, took him into his bank and by the time he was 21 years old had become a partner. In 1870 he was elected to Parliament as the Member for Maidstone (Kent), for the Liberal Party. He was instrumental in assisting through Parliament a number of Acts that were highly beneficial to "the working

classes". In particular, he is remembered for the Bank Holidays Act of 1871, and the Shop Hours Act of 1889. Also, in the same house, from 1952 Terrance Rattigan the playwright lived in the penthouse flat. There is to date no plaque for Rattigan. No 36 was the scene of the murder of Sir Henry Wilson, a soldier turned politician, on 22nd June 1922 by two members of the Sein Fein organisation. Frederic Chopin, pianist and composer, gave his first recital in London at No 45.

At the end of Eaton Place turn right into Lyall Street. Look out for No 7.

(39) The Home Of Thomas Cubitt.

No 7 was built and lived in by Thomas Cubitt the master builder of the Belgravia and Pimlico Estates of the Duke of Westminster. The eldest son of a farmer in Norfolk he worked, at first, as a carpenter and in 1809 set himself up as a master of his trade in London. Six years later he started, the first of its kind, his own building firm. He gathered together workmen from all the different trades needed in the building industry putting them all on the payroll of his firm. This enabled him with his brothers William and Lewis, to enter into the highly competitive field of speculative building. William and Lewis designed and Thomas built large parts of Bloomsbury, Belgravia and Pimlico in London. Later they moved their building operations to Brighton.

At the end of Lyall Street is Chesham Place, turn right and look for…

(40) Home of Lord John Russell

In Chesham Place at the end of Lyall Street there is a plaque on No 37. Here lived Lord John Russell, Prime Minister from 1846 - 1852 during which time he "saw through Parliament" the Reform Bill (Act) of 1832. Names in this particular part of Belgravia reflect William Lowndes, "a political wheeler-dealer" of the seventeenth/eighteenth centuries.

Having made a fortune in developments in the Home Counties he moved into London and began work on high class property in and around Chesham Place.

Chesham Place leads into Belgrave Square where on the corner with Belgrave Place Stands…

(41) The Norwegian Embassy.

On either side of the porch can be seen two samples of Coade Stone. One shows artistic pursuits and the other agricultural ones. A plaque reads "In 1776 these two Coade stone reliefs were affixed to the Danish-Norwegian consulate in Wellclose Square, Stepney. In 1968 the reliefs were erected on this embassy by courtesy of the Greater London Council". Coade stone was an artificial stone made by the Coade Family on the site of where now the Royal Festival Hall stands on South Bank. Unfortunately, for us, the formula was never written down on paper or patented. When the last member of the family died in the early nineteenth century production of the stone ceased.

Walk along the west side of the square to Motcomb Street off which is Kennerton Street, one of the most delightful mews in this part of London. On the corner is …

(42) "The Turk's Head Public House".

Built in 1826 and where a brass plate near the doorway reads "This early Victorian house derives its name from the famous "Turk's Head Coffee House" where in 1764 Doctor Samuel Johnson, Sir Joshua Reynolds, Boswell and Burke founded their celebrated Society. Today, you are welcome to savour the hospitality of this house in a traditional atmosphere akin to that which Dickens, Macaulay, Trollope and their contemporary Victorians enjoyed the pleasures of good company and refreshment". The rare,

but not unique, use of gaslights helps keep the nineteenth century in the twentieth century. The Society founded by Dr Johnson and his friends was the Literary Society. Before entering, look up at the keystones of the windows with the little Turk's heads formed from the colours of the various Rugby Football Clubs. This is a great pub to visit during the "Rugger" season, more so on the eve of an International Match at Twickenham. But be sure you know the winning team for the morrow!

Walk up Kinnerton Street looking for the shop that sells old newspapers and the like, an excellent present for somebody's birthday. Then there is the "Nag's Head Public House", looking like any corner shop of yesteryear, and claiming to be the smallest tavern in the town. Inside it is smallish, but cosy for all that, but the company there has certainly the largest heart. Here come the 'locals' and the visitors alike (those who can find it or have been told the way). For those with time to spare the street, and its many "side-turnings" not more than alleyways most of them, all have a certain charm that is hard to describe but easy to enjoy.

Leave Kinnerton Street by the roadway that leads to Wilton Place and…

(43) The Parish Church of St Paul, Knightsbridge.

Built in 1840-43 to the designs of Thomas Cundy "Surveyor to Lord Grosvenor's Estates", it is of brick and in the Perpendicular (fifteenth century) style. From the arrival of the first vicar, the Revd. W J E Bennet, in 1844 the tradition of the church has been to follow the Catholic Tradition. But, as in the case of St Peter's, Eaton Square, this has not been without its problems. The "Anti-Pope Brigade" made a number of unwanted visits to the church in attempts to force the parish to give up its "popish ways". Bennett resigned in 1851 and went to live in Frome in Somerset where he established the Catholic Tradition once again. This gave rise, in 1855, to the circulation of the leaflet regarding the keeping of the "Roman Catholic Fast of All Souls Day". After condemning the keeping of the service, the leaflet ends with...

"The Church of England ignores the day. The Church of Rome observes it And so it appears does the Vicar of Frome".

So a little bit of London moved to the West Country! There have been a number of alterations to the inside of the church since 1843 that have included extending the chancel and the addition of new vestries. Whatever certain parties may have thought, there was an obvious need for more room for the members of the congregation.

Wilton Place leads into Wilton Crescent which in turn leads to Wilton Row.

(44) Plaque to Alfonso Lopez-Pumarejo.

Opposite the entrance to the Row there is another "blue-plaque" this time commemorating one Alfonso Lopez-Pumarejo of Columbia where he was twice President and also served his country as Ambassador to the Court of St James'. In his own county he is widely known, and respected having introduced a number of social reforms. He died here at number 33 Wilton Crescent.

Walk down Wilton Row. Find on the right hand side a charming cul-de-sac with houses around a large courtyard. Further on can be seen (and visited?)...

(45) "The Grenadier Public House".

Tucked away from the noise and nuisance of London's traffic the pub has a quality all its own - peace! Not that it was always so - because it wasn't quite like that in the nineteenth century when it formed part of the Officer's Mess of the nearby Knightsbridge Barracks. After putting their horses in the stables, behind the pub, they would adjourn here before dining in Mess. One night during a game of cards, an officer was accused of cheating and during the flogging that took place shortly afterwards - he died. It is said that he regularly returns to haunt the place where he was caught cheating... Outside stands a sentry-box much used by tourists to be photographed in, or by all and sundry to shelter from the rain. The signboard proudly shows a Grenadier Guardsman, while inside the walls are covered with military prints and other bric-a-brac.

After leaving the "Grenadier" walk up the steps on the right hand side to the double row of terraced houses. It has been suggested that these were part of the barracks and possibly the married quarters. At the end of the passage, there is an arch. Turn right and follow the way through the archway into Grosvenor Crescent Mews (46) into Grosvenor Crescent. Turn left and at the end of the Crescent is Hyde Park Corner. Turn left once more and walk along to the Lanesborough Hotel (47).

(47) Lanesborough Hotel.

Originally the house belonged to James Lane, 2nd Viscount to Lanesborough and was built in 1719. After a disagreement with their fellow governors several of whom resigned from the Westminster Hospital's Board, a new hospital was set up in the house. In 1827 a new hospital was built on the site to the designs of William Wilkins. In 1980 the hospital moved to Tooting to another purpose built building and finally, the premises were sold, restored and converted into one of the most luxurious hotels in the Capital.

From here a walk along Grosvenor Place (48) will lead back to Victoria Station. Or, alternatively Hyde Park Underground Station is close by, as are a number of 'bus routes.

Keep up to date

If you would like a full list and to be kept updated on all publications available from Morning Mist, please send a postcard with your name and address to:

**Marketing
Morning Mist Publications
PO Box 108, Reigate
Surrey RH2 9YP**

Riverside
From Westminster to Blackfriars Bridge

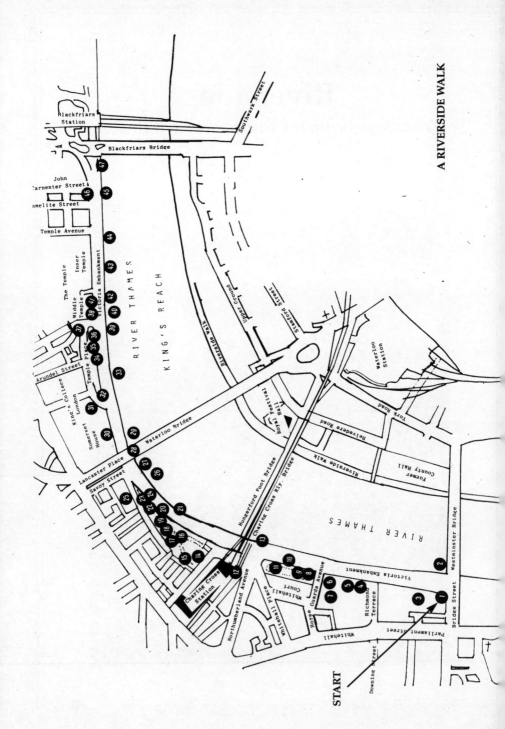

A RIVERSIDE WALK

Key to map

1. Westminster Underground Station
2. Statue of Queen Boudicea
3. Norman Shaw House
4. Statue of Lord Trenchard
5. Statue of Lord Portal of Hungerford
6. Statue of Charles George Gordon
7. Whitehall Palace Stairs
8. Statue of William Tyndale
9. Statue of Bartle Frere
10. Monument to Samuel Plimsoll
11. Statue of General James Outram
12. Playhouse Theatre
13. Memorial to Joseph Bazalgette
14. Stage and seating area
15. York House Gatehouse
16. Imperial Camel Corps Memorial
17. Statue of Robert Burns
18. Statue of Lord Cheylemore
19. Statue of William Lawson
20. Henry Fawcett Memorial
21. "Cleopatra's Needle"
22. Statue Robert Raikes
23. Savoy Hotel Centenary Memorial
24. Memorial to Arthur Sullivan
25. Institution of Electrical Engineers

26. T S Queen Mary
27. Memorial to Walter Besant
28. Waterloo Bridge
29. Metropolitan Police Station
30. Somerset House
31. King's College, University of London
32. Statue Isambard Brunel
33. The "Wilfred" Sailing Barge
34. Temple Station
35. Statue William Edward Forster
36. Statue John Stuart Mill
37. Smith and Nephew's offices, Temple Place
38. Queen Victoria Plaque
39. Memorial to William Thomas Stead
40. H Q S Wellington
41. City's Dragons
42. King's Reach Memorial
43. The Temple Stairs and Landing Place
44. Memorial to the Submarine Services of the Royal Navy
45. Blackfriars Bridgehead Improvement Plaque
46. Sion College and City Livery Club
47. Paul's Walk

Riverside

from Westminster to Blackfriars Bridge

Start: Westminster Underground Station.

Circle and District Lines.

Connecting buses: 3, 11, 12, 24, 53, 77A, 88, 109, 159.

Time: allow approximately 3 hours.

*"L*ondon was born of the Thames, without the river London would not be there today". The River Thames has been both its lifeline and defence in the time of troubles. Along the river have come the invaders from days of old to be firmly repelled by the citizens of London and their allies. In the most recent troubles 'forts' were erected at the estuary of the same river to prevent would be intruders from penetrating further than the end of the line.

London's great river was once much wider than it is at the present time, and much shallower in the past when it could, and did, 'flow softly'. Traders from far lands made their journeys end here with goods that could be exchanged for local products, and then returned to their native lands returning to London at a later date. The Romans realised the potential for this stretch of river, they built London's first bridge to join together the two banks of it. At one end they established an outpost - Southwark as it was later to be called, with Londinium which they first made a trading post and then later fortified it.

With the coming of the Normans in the 11th century, London and its inhabitants took on another character and grew in importance not only in this country but overseas as well. The Conqueror built a large fortress, the Tower of London, to protect his new found diadem in his

Crown. The city began to expand attracting even more trade and people to it, until such time that it quite literally burst at the seams and had to build outside the walls of the City.

Its next door neighbour was, and still is the City of Westminster and between the two there was a roadway that ran alongside the river - The Strand. As time moved on, the land to the riverside began to be developed in its own right, and so the roadway, that once was by the side of the river, became detached from it. This land slowly but surely was developed and built over. First it was the grand houses of the Dukes, and the prelates, with the royals acquiring lands in due season. In the 18th century part of the river bank was reclaimed from the water, arches were built over the mud banks and a housing estate was established - the Adelphi was born. With the 19th century, the Embankment was born under the watchful eye of Sir Joseph Bazalgette, 1819 - 1891, and so, another portion of the riverbank was eroded by man. In more recent times other portions of the riverbank have been 'stolen away from the river' to make man's living more easy and to lessen the chance of flooding at high tide.

But whatever man does, or does not do, "Old Man River" will continue to roll along in full traditional style and will remain one of the Capital's most prized assets.

Starting Point

(1) Westminster Underground Station.

Served by the District and Circle Lines of the network, the station was opened in December 1868 as "Westminster Bridge". In 1907 it was re-named "Westminster".

Leave the station by way of the stairs that lead to Bridge Street. Turn left. Cross the roadway by way of the crossing at the traffic lights, at the foot of Westminster Bridge is...

(2) Statue of Queen Boudicea and her daughters.

The Queen was the widow of King Prasutagus of the Iceni Tribe of East Anglia on whose death the Romans took vengeance on their daughters. It is said that the King had promised the Pro-Curator of Britain much land on his death the Queen thought otherwise! She ransacked Colchester, Verulamium and finally London. In her final battle at King's Cross, she took poison rather than be captured alive by the Romans or tortured. Tradition, rather than fact, relates that she lies buried under Number Eight Platform of the railway station. Thorneycroft 1815 - 1885, the sculptor, has depicted a truly defiant Queen in an acquired Roman Chariot - the spoils of war, with horses without reins or harness to guide them.

Re-cross the road, turn right and walk along St Stephen's Parade, at the end of which can be seen...

(3) Norman Shaw House.

This is the former New Scotland Yard (headquarters of the Metropolitan Police Force) which had been built on reclaimed land following the building of the Victoria Embankment. At that time, the Police were looking for a suitable site on which to build their new offices. The site had been previously selected for a new National Opera House for which the foundation stone was laid in 1875, but the theatre was never built, due to lack of funds. It was on its foundations that the Police erected their offices, with the changing rooms for the artistes being converted into cells of the police station. The architect, Norman Shaw 1831 - 1912, is commemorated on a stone medallion, designed by Sir William Homo Thorneycroft, 1850 - 1925, on the riverside frontage of the building. Built of the finest granite from the quarries of Dartmoor, where the prisoners from the nearby prison were engaged to work the stone, it was used by the Police until 1967 when they moved to new premises in Victoria Street.

Stay on the same side of the roadway and walk along to the first of the four gardens along the Victoria Embankment. Turn left into the garden where can be seen the memorial to the Chindit Special Force of Major-General Orde Wingate, followed by the statue of...

(4) Lord Trenchard, 1873 - 1956.

Born Hugh Montague, he was the "father of the Royal Airforce" which he helped found in 1918. He became the Force's first Air Marshal and, in later years, served as Commissioner of the Metropolitan Police. The statue was designed by William McMillan, R A, 1887 - 1977 who was responsible for a number of other statues and memorial busts in the Capital.

Through the trees and bushes of the garden can be seen the Royal Air Force Memorial to the fallen of two World Wars. Designed by Sir Reginald Blomfield, 1856 - 1942, who used Sir William Reid Dick, 1879 - 1962, for the sculpturing of the gilded eagle which surmounts a globe at the top of a stone column.

The next statue is...

(5) Lord Portal of Hungerford, 1893 - 1971.

Inscribed on the pedestal are the works "One of the architects of victory in the Second World War", at which time he was the Chief of Staff. The statue unveiled in 1975 is by Oscar Nemon.

Walk on to the third and last statue.

(6) Charles George Gordon, 1833 - 1885.

Best known as "Gordon of Khartoum", where he died in the defence of the city against the forces of the Mahdi. He had been sent by the British Government to the Sudan to crush the rebels who had roused the Sudanese against Egyptian rule in 1882. The Mahdi was the Islamic "Messiah". In England, he was held in high esteem as a practical Evangelical Christian, and was a popular hero among all classes of Victorian London. Earlier in his military career, he had been sent to Peking to control an internal uprising. The success of the operation earned him the nickname of "Chinese Gordon". His statue was first erected in Trafalgar Square in 1888, and transferred here in 1953. The general is seen holding a Bible in one hand and his customary cane in the other. The sculptor was Sir William Homo Thorneycroft, R A.

Behind the statue of Gordon are the river steps of the former Whitehall Palace.

(7) Whitehall Palace Stairs.

The plaque describes the stairs as being "Queen Mary's Steps Whitehall", and dates them from 1691 when Sir Christopher Wren, 1632 - 1723, designed a waterside terrace for Queen Mary II, 1662 - 1694. They were uncovered during excavations for a new Government Building in 1939. They have been left in their original position and show how much wider the River Thames was in the 17th century.

Leave the gardens and cross Horse Guards Avenue to the second of the gardens. Here can be seen...

(8) Statue of William Tyndale, c1484 - 1536.

He holds in his right hand a copy of the New Testament, which he translated into English from the Greek, publication of which caused much concern in England in the 16th century. This was a time when only scholars were allowed to read the Holy Scriptures, together with the priests of the Church, in Latin. Shortly after it had been issued, Tyndale had to leave the country for fear of his life. But his escape was short-lived, he was captured by the soldiers of the King, Henry VIII, 1491 - 1547, who killed him. His last words were "Lord, open the King of England's eyes", within a year of his martyrdom a Bible was placed in every Parish Church by the King's command.

Behind the gardens can be seen Whitehall Court which was built in the 1880s to the designs of Messrs Archer and Green in the French Renaissance style. Part of the Court today is the Royal Horse Guards Hotel with nearly three hundred bedrooms.

The next statue is of...

(9) Sir Bartle Frere, 1815 - 1884.

The work of Thomas Brock, 1847 - 1922, it shows Sir Bartle in his Civil Service uniform with open robes of the Star of India. He served as the High Commissioner of South Africa during the Boer and Zulu Wars of the late 19th century.

Continue to walk along the garden path until the riverside gateway. Leave by way of the gate and turn right. Here shortly can be seen another statue.

(10) Samuel Plimsoll, 1824 - 1898.

Plimsoll was an English Politician and social

reformer who is best remembered for his great efforts in preventing ships from being under-manned and over-loaded. In his Parliamentary Bill of 1876, all ship-owners were obliged to mark the sides of the ships with a line (The Plimsoll Line) showing the waterline at the maximum loading level.. He also wrote a book exposing the cruelty of the sea trade in cattle ("Caftle-Ships", published by Kegan Paul, 1890). The inscription on the memorial reads "Erected by members of the National Union of Seamen in grateful recognition of his services to the men of the sea of all nations".

Return to the gardens by way of the gate, noting the "Tattershall Castle" moored by the Embankment on the opposite side of the roadway.

On re-entering the gardens, turn right and walk to the third and last of the statues in this garden.

(11) General Sir James Outram, 1803 - 1863.

A man who served country well in the trouble-stricken India of the 19th century. He distinguished himself during the great Mutiny, and helped relieve Lucknow three times. The figure of bronze, by Matthew Noble, 1818 - 1876, is dressed in a uniform dress coat, behind him is a helmet and mortar. On each of the four corners are placed trophies of Indian arms.

Leave this stretch of gardens by way of a gate opposite the Playhouse Theatre.

(12) Playhouse Theatre.

Built originally in 1882, by Sefton Parry, as a speculation, and in hopeful anticipation that the South Eastern Railway Company, owners of nearby Charing Cross Station, would want the land to expand. But they didn't! The theatre had a chequered life, ending one stage of existence as a BBC studio from 1951 to 1981. In the late 1980s the theatre was bought by Mr Geoffrey Archer, the author, and restored as a live theatre once more.

On leaving the gardens turn right and walk down to the riverside roadway. Cross the road to the embankment. Here can be seen the restaurant ship "The Hispaniola". Open for lunch and dinner - Monday to Saturday only.

Built into the wall of the embankment is the memorial to the man responsible for its construction.

(13) Sir Joseph Bazalgette, 1819 - 1891.

He was the Chief Engineer to the Metropolitan Board of Works among his other achievements was the complete sewerage system for London, at a time when the population was around two million. The same system today caters for nearly five times that number.

From the memorial, walk under the Charing Cross Railway and Hungerford Foot Bridges and cross the roadway by way of the traffic lights crossing. On reaching the other side of the road, walk through the booking hall of the Embankment underground station to the lower end of Villiers Street. Immediately on the right are two sets of gateways. The first leads directly into the third section of the Embankment Gardens, while the second leads to the arena in front of the platform where in summertime bands and other forms of entertainment take place. (14). On the far side of the gardens can be seen the...

(15) York House Gatehouse.

This was once the rivergate to the grounds and house of the Archbishops of York, after Cardinal Wolsey "gave" the former York House in Whitehall to King Henry VIII, 1491 - 1547. It was designed by Inigo Jones, 1573 - 1652, the architect who introduced Palladian architecture into this country in the early 17th century. Andrea Palladio was a 16th century Italian architect whose works Jones had seen on a tour of Italy. It is interesting to note that the gateway is still in its original position, the river is some 130 yards away. The carving on the gate was the work of Nicholas Stone, 1586 - 1647.

Leave the gateway on your left and walk along the north of the gardens. At the junction of two paths stands...

(16) Imperial Camel Corps Memorial.

Troops from the United Kingdom, Australia, New Zealand and India joined together to fight against the Turks during the First World War, 1914 - 1918, in Egypt, on the Sinai Peninsula, as well as in Palestine. The memorial shows a trooper sitting on a camel, and the panels either side - on one side, in bronze relief two men running, and on the other a man standing by a kneeling camel.

Opposite the memorial can be seen the statue to...

(17) Robert Burns, 1759 - 1796.

Born in Scotland, the son of a cottar (a farm labourer living in a cottage attached to a farm in return for farm service). Among his early works, written between 1784 - 1788, while still working on the farm at "The Cotter's Saturday Night", and, "The Jolly Beggars". After the success of the Kilmarnock edition of his early poems, he left the farm to live in Edinburgh. His love of the convivial life nearly cost him his life on a number of occasions. Finally, it did catch up with him in 1796. He is still dearly remembered in the countless "Burns Nights" that are held all over the world.

Continue along the path to the statue of...

(18) Lord Cheylesmore, 1848 - 1925.

Designed by Sir Edwin Lutyens, 1894 - 1944. A stone commemorates Sir Hubert Eaton, 3rd Baron Cheylesmore, over a fountain and small lily pond. He served in local government in the City of Westminster, and as the Chairman of the National Rifle Association. In the latter post, he did much to improve the general marksmanship of the Army before the First World War.

Opposite stands the statue to...

(19) Sir William Lawson, 1829 - 1906.

"A man born before his time" might be said to fit William Lawson. He is recorded in history as being a radical Member of Parliament who encouraged the disestablishment of the Church of England, defended a policy of disarmament, and the abolition of the House of Lords, but only after Free Trade had been established. In addition to this he was a great advocate for the temperance movement. Whoever was responsible for the erection of this statue between Robert Burns on the one side and Sir Arthur Sullivan on the other certainly had a good sense of humour! When his statue was first erected there were four bronze figures around it. They represented peace, fortitude, charity and temperance - they were stolen in 1979, and have not been replaced.

On the other side of the pathway is the memorial to...

(20) Henry Fawcett, 1833 - 1884.

As a result of a shooting incident in his youth, Henry Fawcett was blinded. His blindness is cleverly shown in the memorial. He was a Liberal politician who dedicated his life to helping the poor, being an avid supporter for the "votes for women" campaign. After a short life as an academic, he was the Professor of Political Economy at the University of Cambridge before entering Parliament. Under William Gladstone, 1809 - 1898, he became the Post-Master General, during which time he introduced the parcel post, postal orders and the sixpenny telegram service. The memorial is the work of Mary Grant, 1831 - 1908, and forms part of a fountain the work of Basil Champneys, 1842-1935 erected in 1886.

From here, towards the river, through the trees and bushes of the gardens can be seen…

(21) 'Cleopatra's Needle'.

The monument has nothing to do with Queen Cleopatra VII the Graeco-Macedonian Queen of Egypt who was the mistress of both Julius Caesar and Marcus Antonius, except for the fact that it was erected outside her palace in Alexandria. It was given to England by Mehemet Ali, Viceroy of Egypt in 1819, but did not arrive in London until 1878 when it was erected on the Victoria Embankment. Its interesting history and the story of its voyage from Egypt is clearly told on the base of the column. Inside the pedestal, is a time-capsule which includes newspapers of the day, Bradshaw's railway guide, and a copy of the Bible, with several coins of 1878. During the 1st World War, 1914 - 1918, a German aeroplane dropped a bomb which only just missed falling on the column. It left the obelisk scarred for life however. The height of this granite monolith with $68^1/_2$ ft (21 metres), dates from c1450 BC, and was originally one of a pair erected by Thothmes III outside his palace at Heliopolis. The two. bronze, male sphinxes at the base were designed by G Vulliamy, 1817 - 1886, and modelled by C H Mabey.

The next statue is of…

(22) Robert Raikes, 1735 - 1811.

The founder of the Sunday School Movement in 1780, Robert Raikes is depicted by the sculptor, Thomas Brock, R A, 1847 - 1922, standing with a Bible in his left hand. Born in Gloucester where he helped his father print the Gloucester Journal, he was moved by the ignorance of the children of his parish and set up, in a neighbouring parish, a Sunday School.

Here the children were taught the Catechism as well as reading. Although, at first he met with much opposition by the diehards who disapproved of any popular education programmes for the poor, others were enthusiastic and by the time of his death, the Movement had spread all over England. The statue was erected by Sunday School teachers and pupils in 1880.

Continue to walk along the pathway of the gardens until opposite the embankment entrance to the Savoy Hotel. Here, in 1989, was placed, as a memorial to the founding of the hotel in 1889.

(23) Savoy Hotel Centenary Memorial.

Standing immediately opposite the Embankment entrance to the hotel the memorial an armillary sphere (sun dial) commemorates the centenary of the hotel the D'Oyly Carte Family who founded it, and the Savoy Theatre. Seats around the area make a useful place in which to take a rest, and to watch the "comings and goings" from the hotel. Designed by T Collcutt 1840-1924, with extensions added in 1903 - 04, there are 300 bedrooms. When completed, it offered the most "bedrooms with bathrooms" in London, with electric lifts and lighting added for the further comfort of its clients.

After enjoying a short rest, return to the pathway and walk along to…

(24) Sir Arthur's Sullivan's, 1842 - 1900, bust.

The British composer worked with W S Gilbert to write the "Savoy" operas, "which have now become a British Institution".

The statue and attendant figure of a crying woman were the work of William Goscombe John, R. A., 1860 - 1953, the original commission was for a bust only, but the artist added the figure in order to make the memorial

more attractive - which it certainly does! There is a quotation of W S Gilbert's on the column:-
"Is life a boon?
If so it must befal (sic)
That death when'er he call
Must call too soon".

Continue to walk through the gardens to the gateway and Savoy Place - here can be seen the...

(25) Institution of Electrical Engineers.

Founded in 1871, as the Society of Telegraph Engineers, becoming in 1880 the Society of Telegraph Engineers and Electricians, and, finally, 1888 The Institution of Electrical Engineers. Their objects include the promotion of the general advancement of Electrical Science, and the exchange of information and ideas. In front of the building there is a statue to Michael Faraday, 1791 - 1867, the English physicist, whose discovery of electro-magnetic induction, in August 1831, revealed the principle of the electric motor and dynamo. Built into the wall behind the statue is the foundation stone for the building. The inscription reads:-

Victoria
Queen of Great Britain and Ireland
Empress of India
Laid with her own hand this foundation stone
24th March 1886.

Cross back over Savoy Place and walk to the traffic lights on the Victoria Embankment. Cross over the roadway to the riverside. Here since 1988 has been moored...

(26) T S Queen Mary

Built in 1933 for service on the River Clyde as a pleasure trips steamer, the 260 foot ship was renamed, after Cunard-White Star named their new ship the Queen Mary in 1935, the Queen Mary II. In 1976 when Cunard sold the Queen

Mary she reverted to her original name. Completely refitted, at Chatham Dockyard, in 1987-88, she now serves duty as a Restaurant Ship with bars, a private dining room, and historical display for her visitors.

Facing the river, turn left and walk towards Waterloo Bridge where shortly can be seen the...

(27) Sir Walter Besant, 1836 - 1901, memorial.

The bust and plaque, by George Frampton, R A 1860 - 1928, commemorates the founder of the Society of Authors who was also its first chairman, and who, as a social reformer, was one of the instigators of the foundation of the "People's Palace" in Poplar. The theatre was opened by Queen Victoria, 1819 - 1901, in 1887, as "The Queen's Hall", and was the result of nearly half a century of social reform aimed at bringing education to the poor people of the East End of London. He is buried in the 'new' graveyard of Hampstead Parish Church, Church Row, Hampstead. The epitaph on his tombstone reads "Write me as one that loves his fellow-men" a quotation from "Abou den Adhem" by Leigh Hunt 1784 - 1859.

Walk along the embankment to the short flight of steps that lead to the viewing platform under Waterloo Bridge. Here are seats for the weary to "rest-awhile", with views both towards the City of London (to the left) and Westminster (to the right).

(28) Waterloo Bridge.

The present bridge was opened in 1944, and was designed by Sir Giles Gilbert Scott, 1880-1960. From the platform, it is possible to look through the three arches that span the river. All that remains of the John Rennie, 1761 - 1821, bridge can be seen at either end of the platform. On the riverside there is a bas-relief of the old bridge and a view toward the City of London. Note the old Shot Tower which once stood on the South Bank of the river close to where now the Royal Festival Hall stands.

Leave the platform by way of another short flight of steps, turn right, and walk along the riverside. Over the side of the Embankment can be seen...

(29) Metropolitan Police, Thames Division Station.

The only "floating" police station in London, and probably the world, it is a reminder that the Thames Division of the "Met" is the successor to the River Police Office, and as such, pre-dates the force itself by some twenty years having been set up in 1800. It remained a separate entity from the Met when it was formed in 1829. Within ten years of the latter's formation both river and land police forces were amalgamated. The station is not open to visitors being a twenty-four hour manned co-operational unit of the Metropolitan Police Force.

Continue to walk along the riverside, noting first on your left...

(30) Somerset House

The present building was designed by Sir WIlliam Chambers, 1723 - 1796, and replaces the first House that was built between 1547 and 1550. The site of the house included the Church of the Holy Innocents, and several Inns, but Protector Somerset did not live to see its completion, he was beheaded in 1552. Here also came Queen Catherine of Braganza, the wife of Charles II, 1630 - 1685, in whose time a Roman Catholic chapel became the centre of worship for members of "The Old Faith". When the present building was built, 1776 - 1786, the chapel was demolished. Look for the round-headed archway that was once part of the riverside entrance to the House and gardens.

Next to and yet seemly to be part of Somerset House is...

(31) King's College, University of London.

Founded in 1828, as a competitor of University College in Gower Street "the godless institution". King's College benefactors were the Archbishops, thirty Bishops and the Duke of Wellington. Unlike its rival it had a chapel where, in October 1831, the Bishop of London, Dr Charles James Blomfield, preached on the combination of religious instruction and intellectual culture. The college buildings were designed by Robert Smirke, 1761 - 1867, with a recent wing added in 1972 by E D Jefferiss Mathews. A theological department was set up in 1846 for the training of priests for the Church of England, and in 1908 the College became a constituent college of the University of London.

At the end of the block, where Temple Place branches off from Victoria Embankment stands the statue of...

(32) Isambard Brunel, 1806 - 1859.

The pedestal was designed by Norman Shaw, 1831 - 1912, and the figure by Carlo Marochetti, 1805 - 1868. While still in his late teens, he was appointed the resident engineer for the construction of the first tunnel under the River Thames which his father had designed. He is best known for the construction of the Great Western Railway system, and the Clifton Suspension Bridge over the Avon Gorge at Bristol. In addition to this, he produced the first Trans-Atlantic liners the "Great Western" and the "Great Eastern". The "Great Britain" the largest of its kind of the period has now been restored and is on show in Bristol.

Continue to walk along the riverside past...

(33) The "Wilfred" sailing barge.

Moored at the landing-stage where formerly H M S Discovery, Captain Robert Scott's ship was to be found, the Thames sailing barge "The Wilfred" is now a wine bar and restaurant. If it is open, stay awhile, have a drink and watch the river pass by.

A short distance from the barge there is a traffic lights crossing. Cross over the roadway to the Temple underground station.

(34) Temple Station.

Served by the Circle and District lines of the underground network, it was first opened in 1870 as "The Temple" and renamed "Temple" later. It takes its name from the nearby Temple, the medieval home of the Knights of St John of Jerusalem, an ancient monastic Order which was set up to defend the Holy Land from invaders in the 10th and 11th centuries. Their property (estate) is now owned by the two Inns of the Temple and is where "men of Law and their students" live and work.

Next to the station is the last of the series of Embankment Gardens along this stretch of the River Thames. Here can be seen…

(35) William Edward Forster, 1819 - 1886.

The inscription on the plinth reads "To his wisdom and courage England owes the establishment throughout the land of a national system of elementary education". The Elementary Education Bill of 1870 also created School Boards in order to ensure that standards would be maintained. The sculptor was H Richard Pinker, whose figure of Forster depicts him bare-headed, in a short coat, his right hand behind his back, and a book in his other hand. "Satisfactory, though perhaps hardly rugged enough" is how Edward Gleichen described the statue.

The final statue in the gardens is that of…

(36) John Stuart Mill, 1806 - 1873.

"A life-size and lifelike bronze figure of the great economist and philosopher". He is shown as just about to rise up from the classically designed stool on which he had been sitting. Born in Pentonville, North London, John Mill's family moved to Westminster when he was four years old. Here they were to remain at one address or other until 1837 when he moved to Kensington Square. However, his last years were spent in Avignon, France where he died in 1873. His books and lectures were used by most of the Radical thinkers and philosophers of the 19th century. He was the Member of Parliament for Westminster from 1865 to 1868, having retired from the East India Company in 1858 on a small pension.

Leave the gardens by way of the gateway near to John Mill's statue, and cross the roadway to …

(37) Smith & Nephew's offices, Temple Place.

Built in 1895 to the designs of John Loughborough Pearson, 1817 - 1897, and described by Prof. Sir Nikolas Pevsner as being "a perfect gem of its kind", it was the former Astor Estate Office, with Viscount Astor's flat above it. It is described as being early Elizabethan both inside as well as outside, complete with a staircase in the middle of the hall. Note the weathervane on the roof. It is made of beaten copper and is a model of the ship that carried Christopher Columbus, 1451 - 1506, on his voyage of discovery to America.

Re-cross Temple Place and walk towards the riverside. Cross over to the river turn left and walk towards the Dragons that mark the boundary of the City of London. On the railings of the Temple there is…

(38) An ornamental stone plaqe to the visit of Queen Victoria.

The plaque commemorates the last official visit to the City of London on the 7th March 1900.

Cross the roadway to ...

(39) William Thomas Stead, 1849 - 1912.

This memorial, by George Frampton, R A, 1860 - 1928, commemorates an outstanding journalist who was one of 1,513 people who lost their lives when the "unsinkable" liner, the "Titanic", hit an ice-berg on her maiden voyage across the Atlantic. He became the editor of various papers and embraced Spiritualism to its fullest extent. He wrote books including "If Christ Came To Chicago" and made himself very unpopular with his whole-hearted support of the Boer War. The bronze plaque shows his head in high relief the figures of Fortitude and Sympathy on either side in support. The memorial was erected in 1920 by his fellow journalists.

Before walking towards the City of London's Boundary Dragons, stop and admire...

(40) H Q S Wellington.

The floating livery hall of the Honourable Company of Master Mariners of the City of London, founded in 1926, received its Charter in 1930, and the livery in 1932. It was the first new livery company of the City of London for over two hundred years. It ranks 78th in the Order of Precedence of the Liveries of which there are at the present time (1993) 100 - with two in the wings waiting. The Hall is unique and was constructed by the removal of the engine room, and one or two cabins above deck. The total livery must not exceed 300 all of whom should have at least five years competency as Master Mariners. In addition to the Hall, which has a dining capacity for 108, there are offices, a library and a model room. The shop is not open to inspection by members of the public.

From the "Wellington" it is a short walk to the plinth on which a Dragon supports the coat of arms of the City of London.

(41) The dragons.

The dragons, its twin being on the other side of the roadway, were cast in 1848 for Coal Exchange in Lower Thames Street. When it was unmercifully demolished in 1962 they were saved and, in the following year (1963), erected here on stone plinths to mark the boundary of the City of London.

On the riverside is...

(42) King's Reach memorial.

The inscription reads "In commemoration of the twenty-fifth anniversary of the Accession of His Majesty George V this Reach of the river between London Bridge and Westminster Bridge was, with His Majesty's permission named by the Port of London Authority King's Reach. May 1935". Above the memorial plaque is the coat of arms of the Authority, whose motto "Floreat imperii portus" (Let the port of empire flourish) is inscribed at the base of the arms.

On the opposite side of the roadway are the buildings and gardens of The Temple. Until the building of the Embankment in the 19th century, the river ran up to the garden wall, at which time, the inhabitants had their own stairs onto the riverbank. Today they still have their own stairs.

(43) The Temple river stairs and landing place.

Built at the time of the embankment, the railings guarding the top of the stairs display the coat of arms of the two Honourable Societies (Middle and Inner Temple). A white horse (Pegasus) on a blue background for the Inner Temple, with a white Agnus Dei (lamb of God) on the red cross of St George for the Middle Temple. Here goods could, (can?), be unloaded free of tax for use by the latter day Templars.

Continue along the riverside to…

(44) Memorial to those men who lost their lives in the two World Wars in the Submarine Service of the Royal Navy.

In the centre of the memorial is a bas-relief of the interior of a First World War, submarine's control room. The memorial lists the names of the submarines. that were lost at sea in each of the Wars. Standing like sentinels at either end are the figures of Truth and Justice. First erected in 1922 from the designs of F Brook Hatch and A H Ryan, later additions were made to include the subs. of Second World War, 1939 - 1945.

Continue to walk along the riverside to the, now empty, landing stage where once H M S Chrysanthemum was moored. From here, a good view of the modern developments on the South Bank can be seen and admired (?). The next moored ship is…

(45) H M S President (1918).

The former Headquarters ship of the Royal Naval Volunteer Reserve it is now the home of Inter-Aid, a charity working with young people. "This historic landmark ship is the headquarters training centre of the charity Inter-Aid. Inter-Aid exists to research, develop and implement innovative education training programmes for young people and those who work with them". On either side of the entrance walk-way to the ship there stand the Memorials to the men of the R. N. V. R. who lost their lives in the service of the country in two world wars.

It is interesting to note that the riverside seats along this stretch of the river have "end-stops" of sitting camels with merchandise strapped to their backs. They were the gift of the Worshipful Company of Grocers of the City of London.

Continue to walk towards Blackfriars' Bridge and shortly will be seen on the embankment wall…

(46) A plaque commemorating the Blackfriars Bridgehead Improvement.

"This plaque was unveiled on 8th July 1963 by the Rt. Hon. Ernest Marples, P C, M P, Minister of Transport". The completed scheme won the Gold Medal of the Automobile Association in 1964 for its contribution to road safety.

Across the roadway stands…

(47) Sion College and the City Livery Club.

The college, which was founded in 1624 by the will of Dr Thomas White, who left £3,000 for the setting up of a college for City clergy and an almshouse for twenty poor people, ten men and ten women. The addition of a library as an

after-thought later took over the premises to the peril of the inhabitants living underneath. Under the Copyright Act of 1710 the library became entitled to receive, free of charge, any book published in London. In 1836 this privilege was changed into an annual grant from the Treasury. The almshouses were wound up in 1879, and the College purchased, from the City Corporation land on the Victoria Embankment. The new building was designed by Sir Arthur Blomfield, 1824 - 1899, and officially opened by the Prince of Wales, later Edward VII, 1841 - 1910. Since 1944 the College has also been the headquarters of the City Livery Club. The Club, founded in 1914 provides a centre where livery men (and now women) can meet together to uphold and strengthen the traditions and privileges of the Corporation of London, and of the City Livery Companies. There are a number of sections of the Club which encourage interest and participation in music, tennis, yachting, as well as in motor cars.

Continue to walk along the riverside until a flight of steps appear on the right-hand side this is (48) Paul's Walk. Descend the stairs and walk along the lower riverside walk to another flight of stairs which lead to the subway and Blackfriars underground and British Rail stations.

A Walk with
Charles Dickens

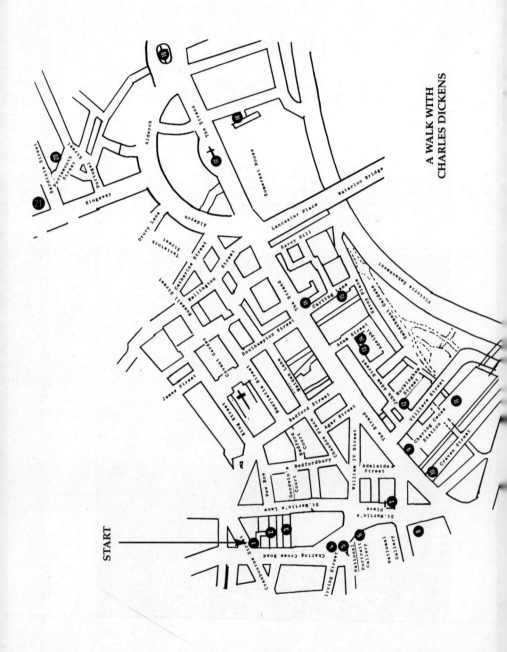

A WALK WITH
CHARLES DICKENS

START

86

Key to map

1. Leicester Square Underground Station

2. St Martin's Court

3. Cecil Court

4. Charing Cross Road

5. Henry Irving's Statue

6. National Portrait Gallery

7. St Martin in the Fields Parish Church

8. Trafalgar Square

9. Charing Cross Railway Station

10. Craven Street

11. Hungerford House and Market

12. Buckingham Street

13. Adelphi

14. Osborne's Hotel

15. Gas Lamp

16. Coal Hole Public House

17. St Mary le Strand Parish Church

18. "Roman" Bath

19. St Clement Danes (RAF) Church

20. The Old Curiosity Shop

21. Finish

A Walk with Charles Dickens

Start: Leicester Square Underground Station.

Piccadilly and Northern Lines.

Connecting buses: 24, 29, 176.

Time: allow approximately 2 hours.

*C*harles Dickens was born in 1812 at 387 Commercial Road, Landport, in the Portsea District of Portsmouth into a "solid middle-class family". His father, John, a clerk in the Navy Pay Office at Portsmouth, was later transferred to Chatham Dockyards and, finally in 1822, to London. When the family moved to London Charles was left behind to complete his schooling under William Giles, who could see the vast potential in his pupil. But, when in 1823 at the age of eleven, he was sent for to join the rest of the family Charles left Chatham and moved to Bayham Street, Camden Town. It was at this time that his father was sent to the Marshalsea Prison for debts, when the rest of the family joined him. All except Charles, who found lodgings in the nearby Lant Street, from where he would travel to Warren's Blacking Factory, Hungerford Steps. (Now the site of Charing Cross Station). This period of his life he carefully records in "David Copperfield". It looked as if his education was to be stopped, and that he would not be able to show to the world his obvious brilliance. However a family legacy cleared up all John's debts and the family were able to resume normal life. Charles was sent to the Wellington House Academy, on the corner of Hampstead Road, and Granby Street, and the time at the blacking factory could be forgotten - at least for the time being. On leaving the Academy, he became an office-boy in a firm of solicitors, changed his place of employment before settling down to learn shorthand with the idea of following in his father's footsteps as a reporter for Parliament. Following an unhappy love affair, he turned his attention to becoming a reporter and as James Grant of the Morning Advertiser (now the Daily Telegraph) wrote "a more talented reporter never sat in the Gallery". Soon his talents were being expressed in other ways notably he had begun to collect together some sketches that he had written for "The Monthly Magazine", and so "Sketches by Boz" was born in 1836 as a two volume book. From there, his literary career was to take off and he was to become one of the most prolific and successful writers of the 19th century.

Starting point

(1)   Leicester Square Underground Station.

Leave the station by way of the exit which leads to Wyndhams Theatre and walk down Charing Cross Road.

(2)   Charing Cross Road.

Shown on early maps as "Hog Lane", and then "Crown Street, it was given its present title in 1887 after the area had been developed around the 'new' Trafalgar Square.

(3)   St Martin's Court.

Mentioned in "The Old Curiosity Shop", published in 1840 with a description of a sick man laying in the Court listening to the footsteps of the passers-by.

Continue along Charing Cross Road to...

(4)   Cecil Court.

The court today has a number of secondhand bookshops and shops where prints from the 19th century can be bought. Like other pedestrian ways in the area the court was used by persons wishing to avoid the Law. It is quite easy to conjure up a picture of the Artful Dodger, in Dickens' "Oliver Twist", 1837 -

1838, using the court to avoid capture.

Continue to walk down Charing Cross Road and look out for the…

(5)   Statue to Henry Irving.

Unveiled 5th December 1910, the work of Sir Thomas Brock, R.A., 1847 - 1922, the statue to Henry Irving, 1838 - 1905, the actor, and the first "man of the theatre" to be knighted, was subscribed to by English actors and actresses and others connected with the theatre in this country. It stands, approximately, on the site of the original Old Curiosity Shop, immortalised by Charles Dickens in his novel of the same name. There have been many, long, debates as to the exact site of the shop, but a lady personally acquainted with Dickens once pointed the site out to Robert Allbut who recorded the fact in a book of rambles in and around London, published at the end of the last century.

Immediately after the statue is the…

(6)   National Portrait Gallery.

Founded in 1856 to collect and display portraits of men and women who are recognised as having made a substantial contribution to British history. It was first opened at No 29 Great George Street, Westminster, but was later moved first to South Kensington and then to Bethnal Green. Its present home was opened in 1896 and was designed by Ewan Christian, 1814 - 1895, which was donated by William Henry Alexander. In Room 17, devoted to the early Victorians, can be seen the portrait of Charles Dickens by Daniel Maclise, 1806 - 1870. The Gallery also owns another portrait of him by Ary Scheffer, 1795 - 1858, the Dutch painter and engraver, but Dickens did not approve of the work. He is reported as saying "it does not look like me… if I saw it I would not know myself…".

Leave the Gallery, turn right and cross the roadway to the church.

(7)   St Martin in the Fields Parish Church.

Designed by James Gibbs, 1682 - 1754, and consecrated in 1726, as can be seen on the pediment over the steps of the front of the church. The Royal Church of St Martin in the Fields was used by Charles Dickens in "The Uncommercial Traveller" which was published in book form in 1860, having been in seventeen issues of "All the year round" previously. "I came to the steps of St Martin's church as the clock struck three". Near to the church in the 19th century there was a coffee shop with an inscription on its glass door. Forster, his biographer, records how Dickens always reacted whenever he read the words. They were printed backwards and read "moor-eeffoc", and sent a shock through his blood each time he read them. Dickens used many of his own experiences of the district when writing "David Copperfield", published in monthly parts between 1849 and 1850, with a book volume also appearing in 1850. In the novel, he has Copperfield describe two of the well known pudding shops close to the churchyard.

Leave the church and cross over the roadway to…

(8)   Trafalgar Square.

Laid out as part of the Charing Cross Improvement Bill of 1826, with the first reference to Trafalgar Square being in 1832 when William IV, 1765 - 1837, made it known that it was his wish that it should take the title of Nelson's greatest, and final victory. It was also the king who suggested that the statue of Nelson should be placed in the centre of the square "such as might not disgrace the patronage of a sovereign and the immortal glories of the hero". Where today the column stands was the site of Golden Cross Hotel so dearly loved by Mr Pickwick and the members of his Club and so well described in the book "Pickwick Papers", first published in monthly parts between 1836 and 1837. When the Rochester coach started from here, there was often heard the cry "Heads. Heads - take care of your heads", from the fact that the archway leading to the street was so low that those riding on top had to take care that their heads were not knocked at the start of the journey. The cry "Heads. Heads..." was that of Mr Jingle, a member of the Club, who often told the story of a young mother, sitting on the top of the coach, eating a sandwich, when her children looked round towards her could only see the hand with the sandwich in it, and no mouth to put it in!

Leave the square by way of the subway that leads to Charing Cross underground station. Resurface at the exit that leads to the north side of The Strand. Walk along to the crossing opposite Charing Cross Railway Station...

(9) Charing Cross Railway Station.

Opened in 1863 the station was designed by John Hawkshaw for the South Eastern Railway Company, and is on the site of Hungerford House in whose gardens Hungerford Market was erected in 1680. The house belonged to the

Hungerfords of Farleigh Castle in Somerset. In the station yard stands a copy of the Eleanor Cross, designed by E M Barry, 1830 - 1880, the third son of the eminent architect Sir

Charles Barry. He also designed the Charing Cross Hotel that forms the frontispiece to the actual railway station.

Walk down Craven Street which runs at the side of the Station.

(10) Craven Street.

Shown on 18th century maps as being Spur Alley. In Oliver Twist, it was here at No 39 that Mr Brownlow came after being removed from Pentonville and as the result of an interview with Rose Maylie, Oliver Twist was reunited. Today the street is a mixture of offices and hotels.

Half-way down the street on the left-handside there is Craven Passage. Turn left and walk underneath The Arches.

(11) Hungerford House and Market.

It was on the site of the former market and house that the railway station was built. A large two-storied building had been built on the site of the house in 1833 for the sale of meat, fish, fruit and vegetables. In the large hall, stalls were set up for the sale of prints, pictures, and other knick-knacks. On the edge of the river were the Hungerford Stairs by the side of which was the blacking factory where Dickens worked for a few months after the move from Chatham to London. It was owned by a relative, James Lamert, who paid him six or seven shillings a week. It was a crazy, tumbledown, old place by the river. His job here, and later in the shop in Chandos Place was to cover the pots of blacking and to label them. This portion of his life is retold in the novel "David Copperfield" when Dickens has his hero working as a labouring hand in the service of Messrs Murdstone and Grinby. Here, too, was the room over the chandler's shop where Mr Peggoty (also of "David Copperfield") slept when he first arrived in London, which were later appropriated by Mr Dick.

To reach Buckingham Street **(12)** turn right from underneath the arches and walk down Villiers Street. On the left-hand side will be found a short flight of steps - these lead to Watergate Walk. Walk along until another flight of steps is reached opposite the York Watergate. These lead to Buckingham Street.

(12) Buckingham Street.

This street, built in 1675, with the surrounding streets are named after George Villiers, Duke of Buckingham, after he had acquired the land in the 17th century and had his new estate laid out. Part of the site was occupied by York House, the former London address of the Archbishops of York, whose Watergate was passed a short step or two ago. For a time Dickens lived at No 15 in some rooms at the top of the house. In "David Copperfield" he writes "they were at the top of the house…and consisted of a little half-blind entry where you could hardly see anything, a little stone-blind pantry where you could see nothing at all, a sitting-room and a bedroom. The furniture was rather faded, but quite good enough for me, and sure enough the river was outside the windows".

Walk along Buckingham Street to John Adam Street. Turn right and walk to Lower John Street. This area is…

(13) The Adelphi.

*The Greek word "adelphi" means "brothers" and it was the Adam Brothers who created, along the bankside of the Thames, one of the most fashionable estates in which to live in the 18th century. Dickens was a great lover of the area, and this is reflected, again in "David Copperfield", when he writes admitting the young David's love of wandering about "that mysterious place with those dark arches". It was in the Adelphi Hotel, now demolished, which stood on the corner of John Adam Street and Adam Street, **(14)** renamed "Osbourne's Hotel" by Dickens that members of the*

Pickwick Club stayed. Here Mr Wardle and family stayed when they visited London after Mr Pickwick's release from the Fleet Prison. Pickwick had refused to pay the costs and damages that had been awarded to Mrs Bardwell in the famous Breach of Promise case. Mr Snodgrass found himself imprisoned in an inner room at the hotel while Mr Pickwick himself suffered the indignity of the Fat Boy jabbing him with a sharp instrument in the leg. Alas, "the Fox-under-the-Hill" public house at the entrance to Lower Robert Street has long since disappeared. Dickens makes mention of the house in "Pickwick Papers" - here he records watching the coal-heavers dancing at the end of a hectic day's work, moving coal.

Walk down Robert Street, under the Adelphi by way of Lower Robert Street. Watch out for cars (there is no foot-path for pedestrians!) and emerge in Savoy Place. In the time of Dickens this was the actual river (bank) side. Turn left to walk along the place until Carting Lane is reached. Here turn right and walk up the lane.

(15) Gas Lamp.

The light from this lamp never goes out, it is fuelled by gases from the sewer system underneath the streets of London. Even when a lorry severely damaged the column an emergency lamp was fixed to a nearby wall.

Continue until you come to The Strand.

(16) Coal Hole Public House.

The 19th century building was a popular venue for those men who made their living hauling coal from the barges on the river to the numerous coal depots which could be found at that time. Dickens makes several references to these hard working men in his books.

At the junction of Carting Lane and The Strand (the Coal Hole being on the corner), turn right and walk along to the approach road to Waterloo Bridge (Lancaster Place), cross the road and continue to walk towards…

(17) St Mary Le Strand Church.

First mentioned in the 12th century, the present church was erected in the 18th century to the designs of James Gibbs, 1682 - 1754, but not before the medieval one had been demolished by the Protector Somerset in order that Somerset House could be built. It was here in 1809 that John Dickens married Elizabeth Barrow.

Leave the island on which the church stands and return to the south side of The Strand. Walk past the Aldwych underground station to Surrey Street. Turn right and walk down the street to an archway on the right hand side. Through here can be found…

(18) The "Roman" Bath.

Dickens probably discovered the bath while working in the blacking factory, or, later when living in Buckingham Street. In "David Copperfield", 1849 - 1850, Dickens wrote "There was an old Roman Bath in those days at the bottom of one of the streets out of the Strand - it may be there still - in which I have had many a cold plunge". The supply of water may have come from the nearby 'holy-well' at the east end of St Clement Danes church but as to whether it was a Roman bath is open to grave doubt. It would have been half-way up the river-bank in Roman times. Possibly it was used as a pure water reservoir by the Romans and by later inhabitants of London. Fresh, drinking water being at a high premium, this seems a likely solution. The bath is today owned by the National Trust, and there is limited access to view. The site is administered by the Westminster City Council who also maintain it. To arrange to see the bath an appointment has to be made, ring 0171-798-2063 during office hours, and give at least 24 hours notice. Or, press the button at the side of

the window to illuminate the interior.

Return to The Strand, turn right and walk along to the Parish Church of St Clement Danes.

(19) St Clement Danes (RAF) Church.

Founded in Saxon times it acquired its suffix after the marauding Danes were allowed by the citizens of London to settle here. Although not destroyed in the Great Fire of London in 1666 the church fell into disrepair and, in 1682, Sir Christopher Wren, 1632 - 1723, rebuilt the body of the church, and James Gibbs, 1682 - 1754, later added the tower and steeple. It was here that Mrs Lirriper, (see Christmas Stories; Mrs Lirriper's lodgings), was married.

Cross from the church to the north side of The Strand and turn left, towards the Aldwych. Walk round until Houghton Street is reached, turn right, follow the curve of the roadway to Portugal Street, via Clare Market. Turn right, cross the road to Portsmouth Street. Here can be found…

(20) The Old Curiosity Shop.

The date on the building clearly reads "Built 1567", and it is certainly a good, restored, example of the type of shop with living quarters above which were built in the 16th century. For over one hundred years it has attracted Londoners and Tourists alike to its doors and the contents of the shop. At the beginning of

this chapter we established where the shop was, near Leicester Square, but still they come in their coach loads to see this building. The maps of the 18th and 19th centuries mark houses as being in Portsmouth Street but only as a part of a terrace.

From the shop it is a short walk to Lincoln's Inn Fields. Turn left along Sardinia Street to Kingsway. Holborn Station is right along Kingsway or left is Aldwych and The Strand.

Keep up to date

If you would like a full list and to be kept updated on all publications available from Morning Mist, please send a postcard with your name and address to:

Marketing
Morning Mist Publications
PO Box 108, Reigate
Surrey RH2 9YP

Roundabout
Hyde Park

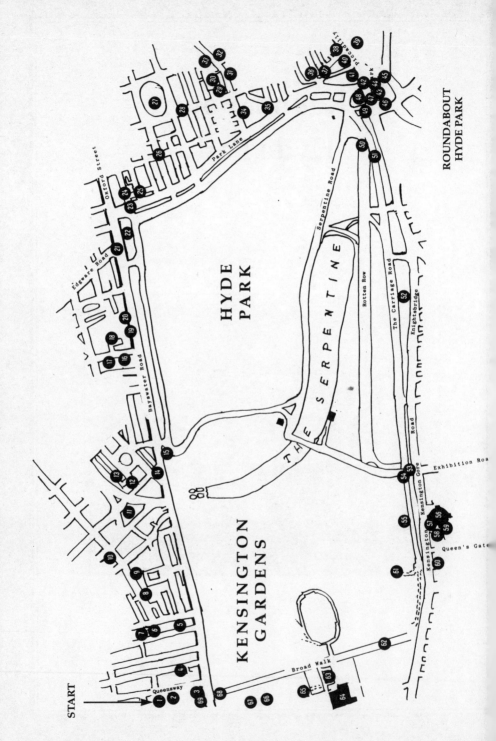

ROUNDABOUT
HYDE PARK

HYDE
PARK

KENSINGTON
GARDENS

THE SERPENTINE

START

Key to map

1. Bayswater Underground Station
2. Queen's Ice Rink
3. Queensway Underground Station
4. Inverness Court Hotel
5. John Loudon's House
6. "Brighton Road"
7. Leinster Gardens Houses
8. London Toy and Model Museum
9. Greek Orthodox Chapel
10. "Tommy" Handley plaque
11. St James the Less parish Church
12. Archery Tavern
13. Bathurst Mews
14. Royal Lancaster Hotel
15. Pets' Cemetery
16. Rajah of Sarawak plaque
17. William Thackery plaque
18. Double Wall
19. Dutch Ceramic Memorial
20. Tyburn Convent
21. Tyburn Tree plaque
22. Marble Arch
23. Park Lane
24. North Row
25. Dunraven Street
26. Upper Brook Street
27. Grosvenor Square
28. South Audley Street
29. Grosvenor Chapel
30. Mount Street Gardens
31. St George's Hanover Square CoE School
32. Farm Street
33. Church of the Immaculate Conception
34. South Street
35. Dorchester Hotel
36. London Hilton Hotel
37. Old Park Lane
38. Rose and Crown Public House
39. Piccadilly
40. Hard Rock Cafe
41. Inter Continental Hotel
42. Subway
43. Hyde Park Corner Island
44. Gunners' Memorial "David"
45. Wellington Arch
46. Royal Artillery Memorial
47. Subway
48. Apsley House
49. Decimus Burton Screen
50. Rotten Row
51. Memorial to Queen's Life Guards
52. Knightsbridge Barracks
53. Alexandra Gate
54. Ironbridge Gate
55. Albert Memorial
56. Royal Albert Hall
57. Kensington Gore
58. Royal College of Art
59. Royal College of Organists
60. Hyde Park Gate
61. Kensington Gardens
62. Broad Walk
63. Sunken Gardens
64. Kensington Palace
65. Orangery
66. Elfin Oak
67. Children's Playground
68. Black Lion Gate
69. Queensway Station

Roundabout Hyde Park

Start: Bayswater Underground Station.

Circle and District Lines.

Connecting buses: 12, 70, 98.

Time: allow approximately 3 hours.

*O*ne of the most popular of all the Royal Parks of London, Hyde Park, comprises 636 acres (257 ha), it is surrounded on all four sides with places of historical and architectural interest.

This walk has been devised in such a way as to allow the walker to complete all four sides on one occasion or, if they wish, to walk one section (side) at a time.

"At the time of the Doomsday Survey in 1086 the area of Hyde Park was shown as being inhabited by wild bulls and boars" (John Wittich, 'Discovering London's Parks and Squares', Shire Publications, 1981). Later the park area was owned by the Abbey of Westminster who used the river here (River Westbourne) as their main supply of fresh water. In Tudor times, the 16th century, Henry VIII (1491-1547), converted it to a Royal Chase stocking it with deer in order that he might enjoy the sport of hunting. It was Charles I (1625-1649), and his son Charles II (1660-1685) who opened the park to the general public, the latter turning it into a popular pleasure resort with foot and horse races, morris dancing and "more elegant pursuit". The park was confiscated at the time of the Commonwealth, Oliver Cromwell and all that while at the time of the Restoration of the Monarchy in 1660 full amenities were re-established. The game of hurling was then introduced which has been described as being a combination of football and all-in wrestling. Both John Evelyn and Samuel Pepys the diarists of the 17th century mention frequent trips to the park, and

describe how the ladies and gentlemen would parade around the park in their best clothes "to see and to be seen".

Today the Park still attracts both Londoner and Visitor alike to enjoy its amenities.

Starting Point

(1) Bayswater Underground Station.

Taking its name from the general name for the area which in turn is derived from Baynard's Watering Place - a conduit taking it water from the River Westbourne that still flows into the Long Water and the Serpentine in Kensington Gardens and Hyde Park, the station was opened in October 1868. The station is served by the Circle and District Lines of th London Undergroun network.

At the station entrance turn right and walk along Queensway. Shortly on the right hand side of the road-way can be seen...

(2) Queen's Ice Rink.

Described as "London's Academy of Ice Skating", it is possible to skate here from 10am in the morning until 10pm in the evening with three separate sessions. Classes are also held during the early evening session.

Continue to walk down Queensway, originally called Black Horse Lane from the local tavern's title, but renamed after Queen Victoria, who used the lane when living at nearby Kensington Palace as a child. At the junction of Queensway and Bayswater Road stands...

(3) Queensway Underground Station.

This too was once called Black Horse Lane Station after the nearby tavern, and changed when the street was altered. Opened in July 1900, as Queen's Road Station it became Queensway in 1946. It is served by the

Central Line of the underground system.

Turn left crossing over Queensway and walk up Bayswater Road towards Marble Arch **(22)**. On the left-hand side of the roadway will be found.

(4) Inverness Terrace.

Until her death in 1873, the Duchess of Inverness, wife of Prince Augustus, Earl of Inverness, lived at Kensington Palace **(64).** *Although married in the eyes of the Church it was not recognised by the State not having been 'authorised' by Parliament. In recognition of this fact she was later created the Duchess of Inverness in her own right.*

Turn left into the Terrace and on the left hand side is...

The Inverness Court Hotel.

The hotel was once the home of "Lillie" Langtrey the actress and mistress of Edward VII (1841-1910). It now belongs to the C G Group of hotels, who allow non-residents to visit the bar of the hotel containing the private theatre where Lillie performed for the King.

Return to Bayswater Road and turn left. At no 100 there is a 'blue plaque' commemorating James Barrie (1860 - 1937), the creator of "Peter Pan". Continue to walk along Bayswater Road to Porchester Terrace, turn left, cross the roadway to...

(5) No 3 Porchester Terrace.

Here lived John Claudius and Jane Loudon both of whom contributed widely to the horticultural world. The small conservatory in front of the house is an excellent example of John's invention, curved glass, that was to be such a great help to Joseph Paxton, (1801 - 1865) who designed the Crystal Palace in 1851. It was John Loudon who recommended the planting of

Plane trees (Planatus orientalis scerifoli) in the London square and street. Jane (1807 - 1858) wrote "The Ladies Companion to the Flower Garden", which sold twenty thousand copies, she also wrote "The Mummy" a tale about the 22nd century which is often compared with H G Wells' "The Time Machine". It was as a result of reading Jane's book that John (1783 - 1843) arranged a meeting between them and that led to their courtship and marriage. In 1825 John lost an arm in an accident while in the following year he started the "Gardeners' World". On his death John was buried in Kensal Green Cemetery.

Continue to walk along the Terrace to Craven Hill Gardens

(6) "Brighton Road" axis.

If the line of this short street were to be projected in a southerly direction it would terminate on the Sussex Coast at Brighton - a strange thought linking London with a seaside resort.

A short distance away from the Gardens on the right hand side of the roadway is a brick wall. By looking over it there can be seen the underground railway lines which carry the Central Line from Marble Arch to Queensway Stations. Beyond can also be seen the backs of the buildings in Leinster Gardens to which we now proceed by returning to the "Brighton Road" and walk through to the Gardens.

Turn Left.

(7) Nos 23 and 24 Leinster Gardens.

When the underground railway system was being extended in 1868 the railway company bought these two houses intending to pull them down. The local residents objected on the grounds that it would spoil the fine row of houses. The fronts of the houses remain, propped up in the rear, and complete with front doors, letter boxes, number plates and balconies. many a new postman has been fooled into delivering mail to these houses!

Craven Hill leads from the Gardens and here can be found...

(8) London Toy & Model Museum.

The award winning museum was opened in 1982 and contains over three thousand toys and models, a number of them are over two hundred years old. The buildings in which the museum is situated consists of two elegant Victorian Villa style houses. In the garden there are a number of working model trains. It is a venerable delight for children of all ages. It is open to the public from Tuesday through to Sunday, plus Bank Holiday Mondays, from 10am on weekdays and 11am on Sundays.

From the museum it is a short walk down Craven Hill to...

(9) No 21 Craven Hill.

Here is housed the Chapel of the Annunciation of the Virgin Mary belonging to the Greek Orthodox Community in London. The garage of the house has been converted into a beautiful chapel for the Community. A request to visit the Chapel should be made at the house.

Continue to walk down the Hill, crossing Craven Terrace with its charming local church school of St James' and St Michael housing over one hundred and fifty children of mixed cultures and backgrounds. Here the Hill becomes Craven Road. On the left hand side of the roadway is Amersham House.

(10) "Tommy Handley" Plaque.

On the front of No 34 Craven Road there is a 'blue-plaque' recalling that the famous radio comedian lived here. "Tommy Handley, (1892 - 1949), was well-known for his radio

programme ITMA (Its that man again) the show that kept Britain laughing all the way to the air-raid shelters during the Second World War (1939 - 1945). Born in Liverpool he worked his way through the Concert Parties and touring companies before finally finding his way into radio.

At Westbourne Terrace turn right and walk along to...

(11) The Parish Church of Paddington.

Consecrated in 1843 when it became the Parish Church of Paddington in place of the 18th century St Mary's on Paddington Green which had become too small for the ever growing population of the area. Dedicated to St James the Less an Order in Council made on the 28th January 1845 (pursuant to Sec. 16 of the Statute 1 & 2 Vic., cap.107) reads that "St James's should henceforth become and remain the Parish Church of Paddington in the stead of the ancient Church of St Mary, Paddington Green". The chosen architects for the building John Goldicutt, (1793 - 1842) and George Gutch (d. 1875). In 1882 the church was rebuilt, except the western tower, to the designs of George Edmund Street, (1824 - 1881), the well-known architect of the Royal Courts of Justice in The Strand. A white marble reredos above the high altar depicts the "Last Supper", with the side panels showing some of the seeds that are mentioned in the Holy Bible. After war damage had been repaired a new stained glass window was installed in the west window of the church. The theme of the window is the Te Deum, the great song of praise often sung during Morning Prayer in the Church. "Te Deum laudamus" - Thee, God, we praise - is a Latin hymn ascribed to St Ambrose who is said to have improvised by him while baptising St Augustine of Hippo in 386 AD. Also in the glass are depicted scenes of life in Paddington, with the Great Western Railway (GWR) being shown, Lord Baden-Powell, (1857 - 1941), the Founder of the Boy

Scout Movement, who was born and baptised in the Parish, as well as Sir Alexander Fleming, (1881 - 1955) who discovered Penicillium notatum in his laboratory in St Mary's Hospital, Praed Street, W2. Among the many famous people married here was Oscar Wilde, (1854 - 1900) the Irish dramatist and master of the social comedy whose "The Importance of being Earnest" is still rated among the most elegant and successful plays ever written. There are a number of items from the former Borough of Paddington's town hall which was demolished in 1965 to make way for the Harrow Road Flyover.

On leaving the church cross over the roadway to Westbourne Street out of which runs Bathurst Street. Here can be found…

(12) The Archery Tavern.

Look up and find the inscription "Licensed Pursuant to Act of Parliament of the 25th of King George the Second". The tavern has supplied not only the local residents well over the past two hundred years, but also in the time when there were open fields here the archers of the Royal Toxophilite Society. Gone are the stables and the old courtyard of the inn but the "House" remains to serve the modern generation of drinkers.

To the side of the tavern is

(13) Bathurst Mews.

Here can be found a number of riding stables, the successors of those who served the tavern in by-gone days. Just beyond the archway are stables of Richard Briggs, while round the corner are those of Ross Nye. Both these stables' charges can be seen regularly in Hyde Park. It was the threat of extinction some few years ago that inspired Ross Nye to approach the vicar of St John's Church Hyde Park Crescent to hold a "Horsemen's Service" in the forecourt of the church. This Service has grown over the past twenty-one years and has been

added to the Annual Calendar of Events for London and its visitors. The service usually takes place on the third Sunday in September each year, when as many as a hundred horses and their riders turn up. Not only do the riders come from nearby stables but often the line-up includes horses from all over the Home Counties around London.

Return to Bathurst Street but not before giving yourself time to explore from end to end Bathurst Mews. On reaching the street once more turn right and return to Westbourne Street. From here can be seen…

(14) Royal Lancaster Hotel.

Opened in 1967 for the Rank hotels division to the designs of the T P Bennett Partnership the hotel stands on the site of the former "Crown" Public House Bayswater Road, and takes its name from the nearby gateway in Kensington Gardens. The Gate itself commemorates Queen Victoria's title of the Duke of Lancaster. A number of gates into Hyde Park and Kensington Gardens commemorate members of the Royal Family and the various titles that they hold.

Cross over Bayswater Road at the end of Westbourne Street, turn left and walk along to Victoria Gate here can be seen, through the railing of the park…

(15) The Pets' Cemetery.

In 1880 the favourite dog of the Duchess of Cambridge died and she was granted Royal Permission to bury it here. Today there are over three hundred cats, dogs and other household pets interred here. Each has their own little headstone, with often "cute" little messages inscribed on them. Officially the cemetery is closed to the general public but by making a request to borrow the key from the Police Station in Hyde Park it is often possible to visit. However, if time is short it is equally possible to peer through the railings and see the tomb-stones. A few years ago a passer-by reported to the police that a body was being buried in the far corner of the cemetery. When they arrived she was duly embarrassed to discover that it was the lodge keeper burying his children's dead dog!

Remain on the 'park side' of the roadway until Albion Street is seen on the opposite side of route. Cross over the Bayswater Road and walk up Albion Street. Here can be seen…

(16) Plaque to Rajah of Sarawak.

Here lived Sir Charles Vyner Brooke the last of the great line of Rajas of Sarawak when their rule came to an end in the 1940s. The family were originally invited by the Sultan of Brunei in 1841 to govern Sarawak on his behalf. With a population, later, of over half a million people and some 40,000 square miles it was a formidable task. One which, perhaps, they were grateful to relinquish in the due course of time.

Further along the same side of the roadway is another plaque.

(17) No 18 Albion Street.

This was the home, in his twenties, of William Makepeace Thackeray, (1811-1863), who lived here with his mother during the time that he was studying for a legal career at the Middle Temple - "a career that he was not to pursue". After the failure of his weekly paper The National Standard he left England and studied art. Later when he returned to London he bought a house in Norfolk Square, a few minutes walk from his mother's house.

On the opposite side of the roadway is an archway, cross over and explore the charming mews through the arch. Here too can be seen a wrought iron gateway through which can be seen the flats of St George's Field's. Note…

(18) The Double Wall.

The area beyond the wall was once the burial ground for the parish Church of St George's Hanover Square. Here were buried a number of famous people including Lawrence Sterne, (1713 - 1768) the author of "Tristram Shandy" (1759 - 1760). Sterne died on a visit to London from Coxwold, Yorkshire, three days after his burial his body turned up in the School of Anatomy classroom in Cambridge. It was returned to London by the next stage-coach. This and similar incidents led to the parochial authorities erecting a double wall around the perimeter of the burial ground. It is said that it is impossible to toss a dead body up and over a wall of this construction without seriously damaging the corpse. Who might be interested in stealing dead bodies, The Resurrectionists who were a group of men who stole fully interred bodies from their graves and sold them to the medical schools, etc, for demonstration purposes.

Leave the peace of the mews and return to Albion Street, turn left, and walk back to the Bayswater Road. Turn left and shortly on the wall of Nos 21 - 23 there is a ceramic plaque.

(19) Dutch Memorial.

The inscription reads "ORANJHAVEN". 'The building served as a club, endowed by Her Majesty Queen Wilhelmina of the Netherlands, for Dutchmen having escaped from their occupied country to join Allied Forces'.

A short distance further on is…

(20) Tyburn Convent.

No 8 Hyde Park Place has been the home of the Order of the Adoreres of the Sacred Heart since 1903. The Benedictine Order was founded by Mother Adele Garnier in Paris in 1898, but was soon forced to leave France under French Laws which made it impossible for them to continue. In the crypt (relics) Chapel is a scaled-down model of the infamous Tyburn Tree (gallows) on which many Catholics and others died. The chapel is open to members of the public on request, and there are daily conducted tours available. In the main, upper, chapel the nuns keep a perpetual watch before the exposed Blessed Sacrament day and night. The Convent is dedicated to praying for the repose of the souls of all those who died at Tyburn. See **(21)**.

On leaving the convent turn left and walk towards Marble Arch **(22)**. On reaching the junction to the road island here is...

(21) The Tyburn Stone.

The stone marks the spot where the Tyburn Tree (gallows) once stood in former times. Standing eleven foot high, and having three sides it was capable of executing twenty-four persons at any one time. It stood here, or nearby, from the twelfth to the eighteenth century and was one of the busiest places of execution in and around London. Here were brought Catholics and Protestants alike. The innocent and the guilty men, women and children shared their end with the murderer, adulterer, highwaymen and the aristocracy. They all died on the Tree. The last recorded execution was that of John Austin, a murderer, who was hanged here in 1738. During the later days of its existence thousands of people would flock to watch the executions take place, to listen to the last words of the condemned, and to cheer or jeer them to their death. A "Tyburn Ticket" was a much sought reward, it exempted the holder from being called upon to perform any ward or parish office. It was granted to successful prosecutors in criminal actions which terminated in the death penalty. The Act of Parliament granting these tickets was on the Statute Book from the late 17th to the early 19th centuries, being repealed in 1818. It was permissible to sell these tickets but not more than once, the highest price being nearly two hundred pounds in the 19th century.

Leave Bayswater Road by way of Exit 11 and the ramp that leads down to the subway. Turn right along the short tunnel at the end of which can be found the Ladies and Gentlemen's public conveniences. Leave the area by way of the double flight of steps that lead to the road island where Marble Arch **(22)** stands. At the top of the steps a bridge crosses the pond with its three fountains. Nearby is a lawn and seats for those wishing to rest at this stage of the walk.

(22) Marble Arch

Standing like a sentinel at one of London's busiest road junctions it was designed by John Nash as the ceremonial entrance to the forecourt of Buckingham Palace. It was based on the Arch of Constantine in Rome, and cost £80,000 when it was erected in 1827. Built of Carrara marble, from the quarries that were used by Michael-Angelo (1475-1564), it was intended to symbolise the victories of Lord Nelson and the Duke of Wellington. Instead the four reliefs by John Flaxman (1755-1826), Richard Westmascott, (1775-1856), John Rossi, (1762-1839), and Edward Baily, (1788-1867), were substituted. The scenes depict Valour and Virtue, Peace and Plenty. The gates, by Samuel Parker, are considered among the best in the country. In front of the Arch there is an open space that is lined with flag-poles flying the flags of the countries of the European Community.

Leave the area by way of Exit 3. At the foot of the steps, turn right towards the underground station of Marble Arch. Just before the booking office of the station turn right and ascend the steps leading to Park Lane **(23)**.

(23) Park Lane.

*Park Lane is shown on early maps as "Tyburn Lane" connecting the site of the gallows with Hyde Park Corner and Piccadilly. In fifteenth century documents it is referred to as "Westmynster Lane", and there has been much speculation over the years that it was a track used by the inhabitants in pre-Roman times as a connecting track between the Harrow Way (Road) and the ford, which is still there, and links the two banks of the River Thames between the Houses of Parliament and St Thomas's Hospital, on th north and south sides of the river. There has been further speculation that the Romans used it up to the time of the building of the first London Bridge as a means of crossing the river. The eastern side of the Lane was not built up until the mid-eighteenth century when a number of large houses were erected. It became a sought after residential road after the 1820s when Decimus Burton built a splendid new set of entrance gates into Hyde Park **(50)**. At the same time the brick wall was replaced by iron railings and new lodges were built at Stanhope, Grosvenor and Cumberland Gates.*

Walk along Park Lane to North Row **(24)**. Turn left into the Row and almost immediately into Dunraven Street. **(25)**.

(25) Dunraven Street.

At no 17 there is a "blue-plaque' commemorating P G Wodehouse (1881 - 1975), writer who lived here. His "Jeeves", "Bertie Wooster" will ensure that PG is not forgotten by any true student of English Literature. His earlier work as a lyricist

working with Gerome Kern has however disappeared into the Archives of Time. Few people remember or know of their work on early musical productions such as "Oh Boy" in 1917 and the great "Ziegfeld Follies" that followed. As yet there is no plaque at No 19 where Lillie Langtry, actress and royal mistress lived in 1877 after leaving her husband behind in Eaton Place. After her affair with Edward, Prince of Wales (later Edward VII) waned she entertained a number of other royal lovers here.

Continue to walk down Dunraven Street to Wood's Mews, turn left and walk along to Park Street, turn right to Upper Brook Street (26).

(26) Upper Brook Street.

At no 10 lived Stanley Baldwin and his wife after his defeat in the General Elections of 1929. His political career came to an end in 1936 over the highly emotive question as whether or not Edward VIII should be allowed to marry Mrs Simpson an American divorcee and still crowned King. He died in 1947 and his ashes buried in Worcester Cathedral near the West Door. A "blue-plaque" in his honour has been erected on No 93 Eaton Square, SW1 Lord Leverhulme, lived at No 39, and Sir Edward Hulton, founder of "Picture Post" once the most popular illustrated weekly magazine in Britain lived, while still at school at Harrow, with his parents.

At the end of Upper Brook Street is…

(27) Grosvenor Square.

The square owes its existence to Sir Richard Grosvenor who in 1725 issued instructions to one of his tenants living in Pimlico to "lay out six Acres (2.4 hectares) of his West One property. Grosvenor Square was born. Standing in the north-west corner of the square is General Dwight David Eisenhower's statue by Robert Dean. He stands "arms akimbo" looking toward No 20 where he located his headquarters during the campaigns of the Second World War. Behind the statue can be seen the American Embassy, built on land of the Duke of Westminster who granted a ninety-nine year lease to the United States of America in 1950. It was designed by the Finnish Architect Eero Saarihen and built between 1957 and 1960. It houses some 700 members of staff in over 600 rooms. On the roof is the massive gilded aluminium eagle with a thirty-five foot wing span and standing eight foot high. It was the work of Theodor Roszak. On the North side of the gardens, that are maintained by the Royal Parks, stands the statue of Franklin Delano Roosevelt, President of the United States 1933 - 1945. The work of Sir William Reid Dick it was unveiled in 1948 by his widow, Mrs Eleanor Roosevelt. Soon after the subscription fund was opened, with a maximum of five shillings (25p) being asked from any one person, the amount was raised and the fund closed. It is pleasant to linger in the gardens particularly in the Summertime when the flowerbeds are at their best. Leave the gardens by way of the south gates. The gates are known as The Diplomats Gates and were erected in 1974 to celebrate the bicentennial of the Treaty of Paris, at which time the separation of England from America was finalised.

Cross the roadway and leave the square by way of South Audley Street **(28)**.

(28) South Audley Street.

On the corner of Mount Street and South Audley Street can be seen James Purdey and Sons, the gunmakers' shop. On the wall there is a Westminster City Council's "green-plaque" which reads "James Purdey the Younger 1828 - 1909/gunmaker/ built these premises in 1880 to house the new rooms and workshops/James Purdey and Sons 1770". There is a further inscription at pavement level that records damage done during the Blitz of April 1941 when a fire bomb fell in front of the building. The various Royal Coats

of Arms' boards displayed in the window show signs of heat blisters.

Opposite the shop is the . . .

(29) Grosvenor Chapel

This unique structure was the work of Benjamin Tibrell the builder and designer in 1730, and is the last propriety chapel left in Mayfair. Propriety chapels were privately built chapels subscribed to and maintained by private individuals. Doubtless this one would not have survived had it not been taken over by the Parish of St George's Hanover Square. When originally built it was intended only for those people who lived in the immediate vicinity, and who couldn't, or didn't want to, worship at the Parish Church in Hanover Square. Sir Richard Grosvenor provided the land and in 1732 he purchased an organ for the chapel. The fine case for the instrument was the work of Abraham Jordan. It has been recently restored and now houses a new organ, the work of William Drake of Buckfastleigh, Devon. At the beginning of the twentieth century Sir Ninian Comper, architect, was responsible for the re-decoration and re-arrangements including the siting of a chapel behind the high altar where the Blessed Sacrament is Reserved in a beautifully designed hanging Pyx. During the Second World War the chapel was used extensively by members of the United States Armed Forces. A tablet on the west front records their gratitude. They might well have been homesick for their native land when attending the church whose design is distinctly Colonial. The burial vaults of the chapel have long since been sealed up, and all records of them, including their exact wherabouts have been lost in the passage of time. Past worshippers at the Chapel have included Florence Nightingale, William Whitehead Poet Laureate 1757, John Wilkes the politician and publisher of libellous articles in the North Briton, and Lady Mary Wortley Montague whose husband was Ambassador to Constantinople in the eighteenth century. While there she introduced the practice of inoculation for smallpox to the local people.

On leaving the church turn right to the north side of the chapel and walk along to Chapel Place North. Here can be found the Mayfair branch of the Westminster City Council's Library Service built in 1894 to the designs of A. T. Bolton. Built into the side of the church is Liddon House forming a memorial to Canon Liddon of St Paul's Cathedral. It is a centre for the pastoral care of young Anglicans, graduates and professional people. Liddon was well-known for his efforts in championing the Catholic revival in the Church of England. In addition, the house is now the National Retreat Centre's offices and it is from here that they organise spiritual retreats throughout the country. Straight ahead lies Mount Street Gardens.

(30) Mount Street Gardens.

The gardens provide a welcome oasis of peace and quiet away from the hustle and bustle of the busy business life outside its confines. Here is a place to sit and read, think or eat one's lunch. Leave the gardens by way of the south gates to the side of which can be seen a memorial stone to the former scholars of St George's Church of England Primary School (31). Founded in 1726 by General Stewart it was carried on in conjunction with the Hanover Branch Schools. Today it is a thriving church school that draws students to it from a wide field.

South Street continues as Farm Street walk along towards the Church of the Immaculate Conception **(33)**. At the junction of the two streets stands the

(32) "Punch Bowl" Public House.

A small friendly house with some interesting prints on the walls. Dating from the eighteenth century it has fought off many attempts by property developers to pull it down to make way for a block of flats or offices. The atmosphere is soon soaked in, to imagine

oneself imbibing a steaming bowl of punch, while smoking 'baccy' from their clay pipes.

Shortly after the public house is...

(33) The Roman Catholic Church of the Immaculate Conception.

A handsome Neo-Gothic building designed by J J Scoles and built in 1849. Here is the London House of the Society of Jesus - the Jesuits, the Order that was founded in 1534 by St Ignatius Loyola to concentrate on theological study, preaching and spiritual guidance, higher education and missionary work. During the English Reformation of the sixteenth century they fell from favour and were suppressed by Pope Clement XIV in 1773 and were not restored until 1814. They are often referred to as being the Black Power behind the Papal Throne. The building is said to have been inspired by Beauvais Cathedral it is entirely open with no chancel arch or screen to block the view from the west to the end of the church. Statues abound all round the church and there are a number of side-chapels. The great High Altar was designed by A W Pugin and was the gift of a Miss Tempest. On leaving the church by the west doorway, cross the road, and look up at the great West Window it is a copy of the East Window of Carlisle Cathedral.

Once more return to South Street **(34)** and walk towards Park Lane.

On the corner of South Street and South Audley Street stands the shop of William Goods, a former tax-collector in whose shop windows can be seen two richly decorated china elephants that are NOT for sale. They were made by Minton for Messrs Goode to be displayed at the Paris Exhibition in 1889. The owners have resisted all offers to buy them.

Cross South Audley Street and proceed along South Street once more.

On No 15 South Street there is a "blue-plaque" to Catherine Walters who lived here from 1872 until her death in 1920. She is described as being the last of the Victorian Courtesans, she was known to her more intimate friends as "Skittles". Across the roadway on a new block of flats once stood No 10 South Street - here lived Florence Nightingale from 1856 until her death in 1910. When she bought the house it cost £3,000. The plaque here is a rare one in that it reads "in a house on this site" rather than "here lived...".

At the end of th street turn left and walk along Park Lane until the Dorchester Hotel **(35)** is reached.

(35) Dorchester Hotel.

The hotel stands on the site of Dorchester House the home of the millionaire R. S. Holford and was designed by Lewis Villiamy. It has been described as being "a private palace of monumental grandeur". Finished in 1857 it was demolished in 1929 to make way for the Dorchester Hotel.

A short walk away is...

(36) The London Hilton Hotel.

Opened in 1963 it rises thirty-storeys and looks over Hyde Park in one direction and the rest of London in the other. Previously the site had been occupied by several houses one of which had been designed by the architect W B Moffat who is best known as the partner of Gilbert Scott. It was here that Syrie Maugham lived from 1944 to her death in 1955. Syrie was the daughter of "Doctor" Barnado, founder of the Barnado Homes for Waifs and Strays. She married, first Henry Wellcome, whom she divorced in 1915, with an alimony of £2,400 per annum. Later she became the lover of Gordon Selfridge who bought her a house in Regent's Park where she met Somerset Maugham whom she married.

After her separation from Maugham she returned to England and set up an interior design practice that introduced the "all white rooms" of the 1920s.

Park Lane continues towards Piccadilly **(40)** and passes between Apsley House **(48)** and Inter Continental Hotel **(41)**. Outside the London Hilton Hotel there is a road from which leads to Old Park Lane. This is the former end of Park Lane. Walk down Old Park Lane.

(37) No. 14 Old Park Lane.

At No 14, now part of a modern office block on the corner of Brick Street, in 1871 a murder was committed by a cook (Marguerite Diblanc) who killed her mistress Mme Reil. The news appalled Mayfair! That such an happening should take place "here of all places!" both killer and victim were foreigners. The former was Belgian and the latter French. Mme Reil, a widow in her forties had, apparently been the mistress of Lord Lucan, the Commander in Chief of the Armed Forces during the time of the Crimean War.

Further down the lane is...

(38) "The Rose and Crown" Public House

"The only public house in Park Lane... such is the boast of the house", is an oft quoted opening gambit by writers regarding this house. Traditionally, the house was one of the last places of call for criminals on their way to being executed at Tyburn. The prisoners were detained, overnight, chained to the walls of the cellar of the house. The house dates from the late 17th century although it has been rebuilt several times since that time. Once the house stood in bleak surroundings, a fact that doubtless made it popular with the authorities for security reasons, but not with the prisoners. It is the latter who are now said to haunt the cellars but they will be the only

spirits as they are used only for the storage of beers - and not spirits. At the end of the Lane on the corner with Piccadilly **(39)** stands the Hard Rock Cafe **(40)**. The Cafe is a very popular eating place in this part of the West End particularly for the young tourists/visitors from the United States of America.

From here, a short walk away, can be found the subway leading to Hyde Park Corner.

*Just before the subway is the Inter-Continental Hotel **(41)** opened in 1975 standing on the site of a number of eighteenth century houses. In one of these houses lived the Duke and Duchess of York with their two young daughters. The Duke later became H M King George VI, whose elder daughter, the Princess Elizabeth, after his death in 1952, became H M Queen Elizabeth II.*

By using Exit 9 cross under Piccadilly to the road island **(43)**.

The Monuments around "Hyde Park Corner".

*Around the Island are several monuments of interest to the walker. Close by the subway steps is the monument to Machine Gun Corps memorial **(44)** known as the "David" statue and with the verse from the Holy Bible "Saul has slain his thousands. David his ten thousands" inscribed on the plinth. Originally the memorial was erected just inside Hyde Park at the Stanhope Gate. In the restructuring of the roadway system here in the 1950s the memorial was moved here. The sculptor, Derwent Wood, has depicted David eight feet high, standing with a sword nearly the same height. Doubtless the sword "belonged" to his opponent the giant Goliath. Dominating the whole scene is the Wellington Arch **(45)**. The arch, a memorial to the Duke of Wellington - the "Iron Duke", was designed by Decimus Burton in 1828 and was surmounted by a gigantic equestrian statue of the Duke. "Mercifully the statue was removed to a parade*

*ground in Aldershot" in 1883. In 1912 it was replaced by the present Quadriga which was the work of Adrian Jones, a retired Captain of the 3rd Hussars. On his retirement from th Army he took to sculpture of which this is said to be his masterpiece. The donor was Lord Michelham, a Jewish financier in memory of Edward VII who had befriended him in his time of need. The figure holding aloft the "Crown of Peace" is an angel, crouching below is the driver of the chariot that was modelled by the donor's eleven year old son. Before being installed on the arch the sculptor held tea and dinner parties inside the horses. On the opposite side of the Island stands the Royal Artillery War Memorial **(46)** designed by Charles Sargeant Jagger who was assisted by Lionel Pearson. The memorial is carved from a large piece of Portland Stone, whose lower portions show carved scenes of the Royal Artillery in action. The whole structure is surmounted by a 9.2 inch howitzer, a strange choice for a regiment well-known for its field guns. It has been calculated that if a charge of sufficient force could be placed in the gun the shell would fall in the midst of the Battlefield of the Somme. It was during the First World War's battle that the regiment lost tens of thousands of its gunners. Perhaps here is the solution as to the choice of the howitzer being a more powerful weapon than the field-gun and could project its shells further and with greater accuracy. At the foot of the memorial lies a dead soldier his body covered by a cloak. Around the base stands a young officer, a cloaked driver, and an ammunition carrier.*

*Standing opposite Apsley House **(48)** is the equestrian statue of the Duke of Wellington by Joseph Boehem that was commissioned to replace the statue removed from the top of Wellington Arch **(45)**. It was unveiled in 1888 by the Prince of Wales, later Edward VII, and cost £8,000 of which £6,000 had been voted by Parliament towards the cost. Wellington sits on his favourite horse, Copenhagen, which he rode at the Battle of Waterloo, and is surrounded around the base of the plinth by four soldiers who represent the four countries* of the United Kingdom of England, Scotland, Ireland and Wales. Soldiers of the Black Watch (Scotland) suddenly appeared from among the cornfields and stopped the French in their tracks. At the Battle of Albuera the 23rd Royal Welsh Fusiliers won the praise of the Duke "just the right men to fill the gap".Ireland's 6th Inniskilling Dragoons led the charge at the Battle of Waterloo, and the 1st Foot Guards who took the last charge at Waterloo against the Imperial Troops of Napoleon and defeated them. Wellington is well guarded by his true and faithful troops.

Leave the Island by way of Exit 8, and on reaching "the other side" leave the subway **(47)** marked Apsley House.

(48) Apsley House.

The earliest building on the site was an inn, the "Pillars of Hercules" mentioned in Henry Fielding's "Tom Jones" as being the place where Squire Western took refuge when his daughter ran away. Later a park lodge was built on the site to be replaced by a house, designed by Robert Adam for the 2nd Earl Bathurst. It was called Apsley House from the Earl's previous title that of Baron Apsley. Little is known about the house except the Adam drawings that still exist in the Library of the Soane Museum in Lincoln's Inn Fields. "The house was bought in 1805 by Lord Wellesley (The Duke's eldest brother) on his return from India; and was in turn sold by him to the Duke in 1817". In 1830 the Duke acquired the freehold and the house remained in the care of the Wellington family until 1947 when the 7th Duke of Wellington presented the house to the nation. Today, as the Wellington Museum, it is run by the Victoria and Albert Museum, and has on display much memorabilia of the "Iron Duke". The present 8th Duke of Wellington maintains a pied-à-terre flat at the top of the house.

Next to the house, forming a triumphal archway into Hyde Park, is the Decimus Burton Screen **(49)**. Erected in 1825 it was designed as an impressive entrance to Hyde Park from Buckingham Palace. The carvings on the frieze, based on one from the Parthenon in Athens are the work of John Herring the Younger.

Enter the Park either through the archways of the screen or by walking along the front of it until a short flight of steps leads into the Park.

Immediately ahead is Rotten Row.

(50) Rotten Row.

Taking its name from the original Rue de Roi - route (road) of the King. Today the way is used by the many horsemen and women who regularly ride in Hyde Park. It was first laid out in the late seventeenth century at a time when the King (William III) was changing his palace from Westminster to Kensington. A roadway was constructed between the two houses. But the road after dark was treacherous, the popular resort for highwaymen and footpads to carry out their criminal practices of robbing and maiming. So, the King ordered that in the winter months the route should be lit. Three hundred lamps were hung from the trees that lined the way. It was the first illuminated highway in England. The bollards (posts) used to separate the walkers from the riders were removed during the Second World War when Herbert Morrison demanded "bollards for bombs". It wasn't until 1990 that an appeal was launched to set up new bollards and the mile length fence was completed by the end of 1991. Now, once again pedestrians and riders are safely separated from each other, except in those places where the walk may cross over Rotten Row.

The road used by motor vehicles - The South Carriage Drive was constructed in the eighteenth century to take the coach and horses traffic of the park. It is often used by motorists wishing to avoid the traffic jams in Knightsbridge.

Cross the roadway and walk away from

the Decimus Burton Screen. Shortly on the side will be seen...

(51) The Memorial to the members of the Queen's Life Guards

The Life Guards were passing here on the 20th July 1982 when a terrorist's bomb exploded killing four members of the Blues and Royals, injuring twelve other people, soldiers and civilians, and seven horses either died or were put down as the result of the blast.

Continue walking along the side of the road either on the footpath or the grass. Later look out for, on the opposite side of the roadway...

(52) Knightsbridge Barracks

There have been barracks here, or close by, since the eighteenth century when premises were built to house six hundred men and five hundred horses. Philip Hardwicke added a riding school with its own stables in the nineteenth century. Walter Besant in "The Fascination of London - Kensington" describes the barracks as "...the calvary barracks on the north side of Knightsbridge boast of having the largest amount of cubic feet of air per horse of any stables in London". By 1960 it was decided that new living quarters were needed for both men and horses and Basil Spence was appointed as the architect. They were not rebuilt until 1967 with various low units culminating with a three hundred and twenty foot high tower block. Incorporated into the gateway in an inner courtyard is the very finely carved pediment from the nineteenth century building.

The route ahead leads to Kensington Gardens. Here is Alexandra Gate **(53)** and the boundary road between Hyde Park and Kensington Gardens. The second set of gates are known as . . .

(54) The Ironbridge Gates.

The gates were made for the Great Exhibition of 1851 that was held in Hyde Park to the right of the bowling greens by the side of the road that runs through the Park. It was by opening these gates that Queen Victoria declared the Exhibition open on 1st May 1851.

Walk through the gates, or the side gate whichever is open and walk towards the Albert Memorial.

(55) The Albert Memorial.
(56) Royal Albert Hall.

Described by Gilbert Scott, it's designer, as "The idea which I have worked out may be described as a colossal statue of the Prince, placed beneath a vast and magnificent shrine or tabernacle, and surrounded by works of sculpture illustrating those arts and sciences which he fostered. I have, in the first place elevated the Monument upon a lofty and wide-spreading pyramid of steps ...". The memorial took twenty years to complete and was officially opened in July 1872. Donations were made from the (Royal) Society of Arts (£12,000); Parliament (£50,000) and the Queen (£62,000). To the top of the cross it is one hundred and seventy five feet high, and there are nearly two hundred portrait figures around the base. Each of the four corners of the memorial represent one of the four continents of the world. Contrary to any rumour that

may be circulating the Prince is not looking at a copy of the Holy Bible - but the Catalogue of the Great Exhibition of 1851. Opposite the monument is the Royal Albert Hall (56) another great national memorial to HRH Prince Albert, Consort to HM Queen Victoria. Designed by Francis Fowke and Henry Scott, it was built between 1867 and 1871, when it was opened by Queen Victoria she wrote in her diary "I had never been at so big a function since beloved Albert's time, and it was naturally trying and emotionnant' for me".The materials for the building include red bricks and terra cotta, the latter producing a continuous frieze around the outside of the building. After the drawings had been photographed and enlarged they were given to the South Kensington Museum Ladies Mosaic Class who made the black, buff and chocolate ceramics with the help of Mintons. Some of the money needed to build the hall was raised by selling, on a 999-year leasehold over 1,300 seats for £100 each. For this purchase seat-holders were originally allowed to attend - free - every performance in the Hall. Today's seat-holders are limited to about 80 occasions, with some "private" events being excluded from the agreement. Of the many events taking place annually in the Hall none attracts more strong support than "The Proms" which were transferred here in 1941 when the Queen's Hall was severely damaged in the Blitz of the Second World War. It is interesting to note that Henry Darrcourt Scott's original name was "Hall of Arts and Sciences", but when the Queen opened the building she added the Royal Albert prefix.

If you have time to search them out, in the immediate vicinity of the Royal Albert Hall are a number of colleges and learned societies.

(58) Royal College of Art.

Founded in 1837 as the School of Design it was originally intended as a school for teaching industrial design rather than the fine arts. After several move the College finally settled in Exhibition Road in 1863 and, on a visit from Queen Victoria in 1896, received the name Royal College of Art. A new teaching block was built in 1961 to the design of Hugh Casson and others in Kensington Gore (57). In 1967, the College was granted a Royal Charter whereby it became a post-graduate university institution empowered to award degrees in its own right.

(59) Royal College of Organists.

Founded in 1864 by Richard Limpus, organist of St Michael's Church, Cornhill in the City of London, after several moves, including Limpus's own house in Bloomsbury, the College was given the National Training School of Music's premises on Kensington Gore. In 1893 the College was granted a Royal Charter, and moved into its present building in 1904.

The walk from the Albert Memorial continues along the path towards the Broad Walk (62).

(62) Broad Walk and
(61) Kensington Gardens.

After Kensington Gardens were laid out in the early eighteenth century by Wise and Bridgman their Broad Walk (62) became a popular place to 'see and be seen' thanks to George II who opened the Gardens to member's of the public on Saturdays, if the Court was out of London at Richmond, and provided they were always respectably dressed. The trees that once stood either side of the Walk were, by tradition, laid out to reproduce the Brigade of Guards position at the Battle of Blenheim in 1704. In the 1950s all the elm trees were found to be suffering from "Elm-tree disease" and were cut down. They were replaced by oak and copper beech trees in 1953.

Porceed up the Walk noting on the way…

The statue of Queen Victoria.

Placed here by her daughter Princess Louise a talented sculptor who, because of her royal connections, has not enjoyed the recognition that she truly deserved. The Queen, seated on a Chair of State wearing her Coronation robes and bearing in her right hand the Sceptre, was unveiled by Edward, Prince of Wales in June 1893. It was commissioned and given by the People of Kensington as part of their Golden Jubilee Celebrations.

On the opposite side of the Broad Walk can be seen the Round Pond that was "filled with water in 1728". It became a favourite place for George II to take his constitutional walk around each morning. In actual fact, the shape of the pond is not round, but more like that of a Tudor Rose. On each of the four "sides" there can be detected inlets in the banks of the pond. Queen Victoria allowed miniature square riggers to sail on it ... "scattering the ducks there". When drained for cleaning the seven acre pond reveals innumerable bottles and dogs' leashes that have been thrown in the pond.

Continue to walk up the Broad Walk where on the left hand side there is a path, turn off the Walk and find...

(63) The Dutch or Sunken Garden.

It is impossible to describe other than it being a field of floral delight throughout the flowering seasons of the year. Alas, in the Great Hurricane Storm of 1987 the green vaulted cloisterlike walk around the side of the garden was severely damaged and had to be taken down. But the side "walls" still allow visitors to peep through the "portholes" into the garden itself. At any time of the year a detour from the Broad Walk is enhanced by coming here.

(65) The Orangery.

Between 1702 and 1705 the Orangery was built to the designs of Wren (?), and/or Vanburgh or Hawksmoor. Sufficient to record that Wren is given as the official architect in the guide but that both Vanburgh and Hawksmoor were closely involved with him on a number of

occasions. No oranges have ever been successfully grown here but the building's acoustics are perfect for small groups of musicians to play in and for the public to enjoy, away from the hustle and bustle of the twentieth century. The statues inside are attributed to Francavilla and the classical-style urns by Caius Gabriel Cibber and Edward Pearce.

Return, once more, to the Broad Walk and walk along to the Children's Playground (68) and the Elfin Oak (67). Here too is a refreshment kiosk.

(66) The Elfin Oak and
(67) The Childrens Playground.

Originally growing in Richmond Park the Elfin Oak (66) stump was carved by Ivor Innes with all the delightful figures of fairies and elves with their little animal friends. In order to protect them from little and large human hands, a railing has been erected around the oak - but that does not spoil the viewing in any way at all.

James Barrie the creator of "Peter Pan" lived not far away in the Bayswater Road and was one of the first members of the public to be given a key to the Gardens before the general public were allowed in other than Sundays. His love for children led him to have created a playground (67) here for children. The children of today can safely play on the innumerable swings, roundabouts, etc, that are to be found here - under supervision.

We leave Kensington Gardens at the end of the Broad Walk by way of the Black Lion Gate (68). The gate takes its name from a former tavern in the Bayswater Road that also gave its name to Black Lion Lane - now Queensway.

Directly across the Bayswater Road is Queensway Underground Station (69) and a short walk up Queensway brings the walker back to Bayswater Underground Station (1) from where the walk began.

Soho

Past and Present

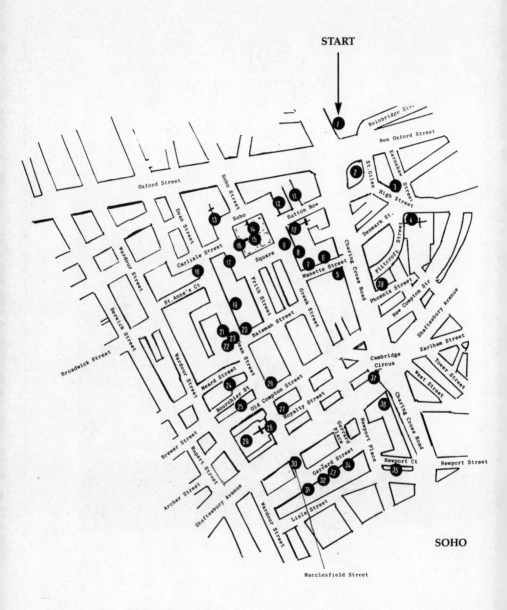

START

Rainbridge Str:

New Oxford Street

Oxford Street

Soho Street

St.Giles

Earnshaw Street

High Street

Denmark St.

Dean Street

Carlisle Street

Soho

Sutton Row

Manette Street

Charing Cross Road

Filicroft Street

Phoenix Street

New Compton Str

Shaftesbury Avenue

Square

St.Anne's Ct.

Frith Street

Greek Street

Earlham Street

Wardour Street

Berwick Street

Bateman Street

Broadwick Street

Dean Street

Meard Street

Cambridge Circus

Tower Street

West Street

Charing Cross Road

Bourchier St

Old Compton Street

Royalty Street

Newport Ct.

Newport Street

Brewer Street

Rupert Street

Gerrard Place

Newport Place

Gerrard Street

Archer Street

Macclesfield Street

Shaftesbury Avenue

Wardour Street

Lisle Street

SOHO

114

Key to map

1. Dominion Theatre
2. Centre Point
3. The Conservatory
4. St Giles' in the Fields Parish Church
5. Foyles Bookshop
6. Former Workhouse
7. Chapel of St Barnabas
8. House of St Barnabas
9. Soho Square
10. St Patrick's Roman Catholic Church
11. Falconberg Mews and Court
12. Speaker Onslow Plaque
13. French Protestant Church in London
14. Charles II Statue
15. "Summer House"
16. West Gates
17. No. 38 Soho Square
18. Nellie Dean Public House
19. Leoni's Restaurant
20. The Crown and Two Chairmen Public House
21. Office of the Board of the Green Cloth
22. Royalty House
23. Home of James Thornhill
24. Meard Street Houses
25. Bourchier Street
26. Groucho Club
27. The French House
28. St Anne's Parish Church
29. St Anne's Gardens
30. Macclesfield Street
31. Chinese Stone Lions
32. Edmund Burke Plaque
33. Paul de Lamerie Plaque
34. John Dryden Plaque
35. Newport Court Shops
36. Limelight
37. Palace Theatre
38. Phoenix Theatre

Soho – *Past and Present*

Start: Tottenham Court Road.

Northern and Central Lines.

Connecting buses: 7, 8, 10, 14A, 22B, 24, 25, 29, 38, 55, 73, 98, 134, 176.

Time: allow approximately 3 hours.

*T*oday's Soho has a mixed reputation of being the "home" of sex-shows and good restaurants, but human and animal flesh are only two of the commodities on sale here! The whole of the area is a maze of narrow side streets, courtyards and dark alleys. Soho has long been the refuge of refugees from all over Europe. A "European Community" was set up here long before the Treaty of Rome and the setting up of a bureaucracy in Brussels. Records show that in 1562 the "Mayor, Aldermen and other worshipful persons" came to the area to hunt wild hare before returning to the City for dinner. It is likely that the area acquired its name from the call of these hare hunters "so-ho, so-ho, so-ho!" The cry was the English version of the French "Tally-ho" which became so unpopular during the seventeenth century. It was during that same century that the land was bought by the Duke of Monmouth who had a large mansion built for himself here on the south side of the square. It is to the same Duke that many writers attribute the name "Soho" to this area. The word was used as a password during the Battle of Sedgemoor, the last battle fought on English soil in 1685. It seems more likely that the Duke used the word because of his London home being sited in the former hunting area.

Starting Point: Dominion Theatre outside Tottenham Court Road Station.

(1)   Dominion Theatre outside Tottenham Court Road Station.

The site of the theatre marks the place where Meux's Brewery once stood. Here, too, in earlier times could be found the gallows, road junctions being a favourite place to erect them (as a warning to other would-be offenders of the Law), and the village pound for stray animals. The Brewery had an enormous vat capable of holding over three thousand gallons. On one occasion in 1814 when it was full of porter, the vat burst and the nearby rookery was flooded. The inhabitants were, for the main, felons of some sort or other who had banded together in a kind of ghetto for their own safety. By the end of the night, it is recorded, there was not one single sober person in the vicinity. The local parson on a late night sick-call joined in the revelry of his parishioners. Next to the theatre once stood the "Horseshoe Hotel", which took its name from an earlier tavern on the site. This, in turn, acquired the name from either a smithy that once was here, or from the shape of the dining room table. History does not record which of the answers are the correct one.

Turn away from the theatre and walk to New Oxford Street, turn left, and cross the roadways, by way of the traffic lights crossing just before Bainbridge Street. Pass under the building that bridges the road. Pause and look up at…

(2)   Centre Point.

Built to the designs of Richard Seifert and Partners in the early 1970s it soon became "a true London landmark" from the start. At the same time it acquired a "scandalous reputation" as being unoccupied for a large number of years. Although the small block of flats attached to the building were let, the main building could only attract squatters from time to time. Today's tenants of this multi-storied building is the Confederation of British Industry (CBI). Before they took a lease on the building it had been suggested that the British (Museum) Library should occupy it. But it was found to be inconvenient for the library.

The way ahead is through St Giles's High Street leading to the Parish Church of Saint Giles in the Fields. Opposite the church stands...

(3) "The Conservatory".

Standing on the site of the "White Hart Tavern". It was from the tavern that criminals on their way to be executed at Tyburn Tree were given a bowl of soup or ale, according to the season, as a last act of charity.

Cross the roadway to...

(4) The Parish Church of St Giles's in the Fields.

This is the third church on the site and was erected in 1734 from the designs of Henry Flitcroft, a protégé of Lord Burlington and a pupil of James Gibbs. It is Palladian in style, Flitcroft took the work of Andreas Palladio, a sixteenth century Italian architect, as his model. Externally the building gives no indication of the splendour of the interior with its ornate barrel-vaulted ceiling and colour scheme of blue-grey, red and gold. The pulpit came from the nearby former West Street Chapel which was the first purpose built chapel for the followers of John and Charles Wesley. On the north side of the church were buried, after their execution at Tyburn, a number of Roman Catholic Christians. Amongst those buried here were most of those involved in the "Popish Plot", five Jesuits (members of the Society of Jesus), and the mutilated remains of Oliver Plunkett Archbishop of Armagh and Primate of Ireland. Charles II personally ordered that the archbishop should be decently placed in a coffin. The inscription on it read "In this tomb resteth the body of the Right Reverend Oliver Plunkett, Archbishop of Armagh and Primate of Ireland, who in hatred of religion was accused of high treason by false witnesses, and for the same condemned and executed at Tyburn, the first of July 1681, in the reign of Charles II". His body now lies

buried at Downside Abbey, Bath, and his head in Drogbede in Ireland. The seventeenth century "Last Judgement", above the archway at the west end of the churchyard, is a fibre-glass copy of the original that for safety has now been attached to the wall in the north west corner of the church.

On leaving the church walk along Denmark Street, known to many as the "Tin Pan Alley" of London, until Charing Cross Road. Cross over the road by way of the traffic lights and find . . . Manette Street **(5)** on one corner of which is Foyles, whose boast has always been that it is the largest bookshop in London. On the opposite corner is also a bookshop – Waterstone's. On the right-hand side of the street there is...

(6) A former parish workhouse.

*Built in the eighteenth century to the designs of James Paine and a reflection of the need, yesterday as much as today, to look after the wanderer and the homeless, as well as the poor and needy. Parish records throughout London and its former villages recall the giving of money to persons not resident in the parish in order that they may be persuaded "to pass on to another parish". The street's name calls to mind that Doctor Manetter, one of Charles Dickens characters in the "Tale of Two Cities" lived in a house nearby. Next to this building can be seen the Chapel of the House of St. Barnabas **(7)**. To visit the chapel application must be made at the house.*

At the end of Manette Street pass under the building over the roadway in Greek Street. Turn right. On the next corner is the House of St Barnabas **(8)**.

(8) The House of St Barnabas.

The House, No. 1 Greek Street, was built in 1746 and has been described as "the last remaining house in which are preserved the magnificent delights of eighteenth century Soho Square". Richard Beckford, the younger brother of William Beckford, Lord Mayor of London in 1762 and 1769, was the first occupant of the house. Various private persons lived here until 1862 when the "House of Charity for Distressed Women in London" that had been founded in 1846 in Rose (now Manette) Street moved into larger premises here. Visits to the house can be arranged preferably with prior notice.

Greek Street leads directly into…

(9)   Soho Square.

First laid out by Gregory King, and called King Square until the mid-eighteenth century after its builder. William Maitland, the London historian, wrote in his diary "the stately quadrate… denominated King's Square… vulgarly known as Soho Square". In some seventeen-thirties drawings both names are freely used. It became one of the most fashionable places in London to have a house from the time of its conception until well into the nineteenth century. To learn something of the Pre-Second World War Soho read Graham Greene's "Brighton Rock" with its stories of "razor-gangs" and "the girls". On the corner of Sutton Row stands the Roman Catholic Church of St Patrick (10), built on the site of a house lived in by Cassanova's "bosom companion" Madame Cornelys. This notorious house was demolished in 1788, except the ballroom, this was "converted" into the first chapel on this side of the square. It was the first Catholic chapel or church not attached to an Embassy since the Reformation in the sixteenth century The church that now stands here was built in 1893 to the designs of John Kelly. it is a popular church for "catholic society weddings" and attracts many others to its services. The Presbytery, next door to the church, also houses the Chinese Catholic Centre.

To the side of the church runs Sutton Row and, with Falconberg Mews and Court (11)

are all reminders of the Thomas Lord Fauconberg of Sutton Court, Chiswick who lived here with his wife Mary the third daughter of Oliver Cromwell. To continue, walk along the east side of the square where on No 20 (12) can be seen the…

(12)   Plaque to Arthur Onslow and
(13)   The French Protestant Church.

Arthur Onslow was the Speaker of the House of Commons for thirty-three years where he was known for "his independence and impartiality". He lived in the square for nineteen years before retiring to Great Russell Street, where he died in 1768. On the North side of the square can be seen two late seventeenth century houses, complete with their original staircases, although much else in them has been disposed of over the past few years. In the north-west corner of the square is the French Protestant Church in London (13) founded in 1550 by a Royal Charter of Edward VI and who, after using various places as their "home", finally settled here in 1893 by Aston Webb, the architect. The noticeboard proudly proclaims, in French, that all are welcome to attend its Sunday Morning services.

Return to Soho Street on the north side of the square, cross the road and explore the gardens. Here can be seen…

(14)   Caius Cibber's statue of
Charles II.

Originally the centrepiece of the gardens when it was mounted on a pedestal in the middle of a fountain. In each of the four corners were symbolic figures representing the four great rivers of England - viz. the Thames, the Severn, the Tyne and the Humber. According to the London historian Edward Walford the south side of the base of the statue, now at Grims Dyke Harrow Weald, was adorned with "the figure of an old man and a young virgin, with the stream of the fountain ascending: on the west side lay a naked virgin (only nets draped about her) reposing on a fish, out of whose mouth flowed a stream of water: on the north side, there was an old man recumbent on a coal-bed, and an urn in his hand whence issued a stream of water: on the east side rested a very aged man, with water running from a vase and his right hand lain upon a shell".

(15) The Gardeners' Shed.

This building now in the centre of the square was designed by S J Thacker between 1875 and 1876 which was described by the late Nikolas Pevsner as being a "silly half-timbered summer house" and is used as the gardeners' shed. It also acts as a ventilation shaft for an electric transformer station. By placing one's hands against the wooden supports it is often possible to feel the vibrations of the transformer.

Leave the gardens by way of the west gate **(16)** across the road to the left is…

(17) No 36 Soho Square.

A typical eighteenth century house with an excellent example of a fan-light of the period over the doorway. Note the wrought-iron guard behind the fan-like windows, an early security measure to prevent the would-be burglars from breaking into the house by way of the fan-light. On the corner of the square and Carlisle Street stands Carlisle House, designed by John Sanger in 1735, it has a porch at the entrance that enabled sedan chairmen to put down their chair in wet weather here so that their passenger did not have to go into the open air.

Walk along Carlisle Street to Dean Street on the opposite corner can be seen…

(18) The "Nellie Dean" Public House.

The Pub's signboard showing a handsome lady whose face would arouse any gentleman worth his salt to burst into the song "Sweet Nellie Dean", although the lady of the sign does not look as if she had ever been by the stream of the song! The Dean of Dean Street is not the good lady but Dean Compton of the seventeenth century who later was to become the Bishop of London.

Walk down Dean Street to…

(19) No 26 Leoni's.

At No 26 is the famous Italian restaurant Leoni's whose famous remark has made the history books. "My kitchen's are not as clean as the Savoy Hotel's. The Savoy Hotel's are as clean as mine!". The "blue-plaque" on the outside of the building commemorates Karl Marx and his family living here in the middle of the nineteenth century. While living here he wrote his famous "Das Kapital" statement on Communism.

On the corner of Dean Street and Bateman Street stands…

(20) "The Crown and Two Chairmen" Public House.

The pub achieved "fame and 'royal' title" after Queen Anne had her portrait painted by James

Thornhill in his house on the opposite side of the road. Traditionally, her sedan chair bearers rested here while the artist was at work in his studio. Later the upper room of the house was used as a club, of which Thackeray was a member. George Augusta Sala, the journalist, claimed that he first met Thackeray in this "place of refreshment", presumably this was prior to his becoming "one of the sights" of Fleet Street.

Cross over the roadway to...

(21) No 78.

No 78 are the offices of Allen and Fraser solicitors established in 1788, it is also the Clerk's Office of the Board of the Green Cloth Verge of the Palaces. This Board is responsible for the licensing of all the public houses whose premises border onto the land of the Royal Palaces. It meets once a year, in February, consists of the Master of the Household and five other persons. They issued licences annually to these establishments.

(22) No 74 was the home of James Thornhill at the time that he was painting the portrait of Queen Anne, and at which time William Hogarth eloped with Sir James's daughter. William and James Thornhill were married in the old Parish Church of Paddington on the Green.

Continue down Dean Street and later make a short detour right down... **(24)** Meard Street with its row of eighteenth century houses making them one of the most rewarding set of residences in the Soho of today.

Return to Dean Street and turn right. Walk on to the next street.

(25) Bourchier Street.

Bourchier Street is shown on nineteenth century maps as Little Dean Street. In 1936 during the time of the renaming of many of

London's streets, it became Bourchier Street in memory of the Revd Basil Bourchier, the Rector of the nearby Parish Church of St Anne's Soho. He died in 1934.

On the opposite side of the road is...

(26) No 45 is the Groucho Club (London), a rendezvous for publishers and the literary world.

Continue down Dean Street and cross over Old Compton Street to arrive at...

No 48 is the former "York Minster" public house, now, more appropriately named the "French House" being the best place in London to celebrate Bastille Day on the 14th July each and every year. The house was a meeting place during the Second World War for members of the Resistance, when they were in London! and the Free French Forces led by Generalle Charles De Gaulle. The general was a frequent visitor here during that time of strife. Today, the clientele consists mainly of film-writers, and their associates, publishers and writers and, of course, Frenchmen. It is hardly surprising to note that more wine is drunk here than beer!!

Across the roadway is the newly rebuilt Parish Church of St Anne's Soho **(28)**. Destroyed except for the walls and the tower during the Blitz of 1940-1941, the new church and church complex was consecrated in 1991.

Return to Old Compton Street and turn left. At the end of the street turn left and shortly there will be St Anne's Gardens **(29)**.

(29) St Anne's Gardens.

All that is left of the churchyard of St Anne's has now been turned into a public open space for all to enjoy and to rest in. On the base of the tower are two interesting inscriptions. First, the former tombstone of Theodore King of Corsica, he was a German baron and served in the Swedish Army. In 1736 he was offered the Throne of Corsica and by reputation was a well-liked and able ruler but… he did not have the money to pay his army. He came to England to seek a fortune - but failed in his quest. Subsequently, he was declared insolvent and offered his kingdom to his creditors. He died in 1756, a pauper, and was buried here in the churchyard through the benevolence of a nearby oilman. Second, under the central window of the church tower there is a memorial inscription to David Williams, the Founder of the (Royal) Literary Fund in 1790, who is buried here. Inside the tower are the ashes of Dorothy L Sayers, the great detective story writer, who in the 1950s was the Churchwarden of St Thomas's Regent Street. St Thomas' and St Anne's Parish have since been united.

Leave the gardens. Turn left and walk along to Shaftesbury Avenue. Cross the road by way of the crossing by the traffic lights. Turn left and walk along to…

(30) Macclesfield Street.

Charles Gerard, first Earl of Macclesfield had a house built here c1681, on land that had previously been held by Henry, Prince of Wales the son of James I. Faithorne and Newcourt's map of 1658 indicates that there was an enclosed area here as a Military Ground. Records show the Earl seized it in 1661 and threatened the "Members of the said Company that he would cut them to the ground if they ever tried to return". This was no idle remark the Earl had his own "lawless bands of Civil War veterans" at his personal command. In the early 1680s he had built, in Gerrard Street of today, a fine mansion where he and his successors lived until well into the eighteenth century. It is interesting to note that the street signs hereabouts are in English and Chinese.

The way ahead is through the Chinese Gateway to Gerrard Street and London's China Town.

(31) The Chinese Lions.

Here stand a pair of stone Chinese Lions, the gift of the People's Republic of China, which

were unveiled by HRH the Duke of Gloucester in 1985, during the celebration of the four-hundredth anniversary of the City of Westminster. Also present were the Head Ambassador of the People's Republic of China, the Lord Mayor of Westminster, the Hong Kong Commissioner and the President of the China Town Chinese Association (London) .

Leave the two lions to the right and walk along Gerrard Street. Whilst walking look out for...

(32) Plaque to Edmund Burke.

At No 37 is a (Royal) Society of Arts plaque commemorating Edmund Burke, statesman, author and philosopher who lived here between 1787 to 1790. He championed in Parliament the cause of Catholic Emancipation and free trade with Ireland. As an author he is best known for his "Reflections on the French Revolution".

(33) No 40, here is a green plaque of the Westminster City Council and the Worshipful Company of Goldsmiths of the City of London commemorating Paul de Lamerie, 1688 - 1751.

(34) Nos 42 - 44 the (Royal) Society of Arts, "blue and white plaque" on the building commemorates John Dryden, poet and dramatist and his residence in this street.

Shortly after this plaque there is another Chinese Gateway leading to Newport Place and then Newport Court, between which there is an overspill from Gerrard Street with more Chinese shops.

(35) Newport Court.

Newport Court passes through where, in the seventeenth century, Newport House had stood. Today, one side of the court is made up of a variety of shops in early nineteenth century buildings while the opposite side comprises of a modern development of shops and flats that stretch to Charing Cross Road.

On reaching the end of the court turn left and walk up Charing Cross Road - the home of many bookshops selling secondhand books. Just before the junction with Cambridge Circus is...

(36) The Limelight.

The Limelight - "a contemporary venue" offering facilities that can cater for all types of functions from dinner/dances to fashion shows. It boasts of having all the latest technology to enhance its clients needs. It was built originally to the designs of James Cubitt for the Welsh Presbyterian Church in 1888 whose congregations it served until the 1980s. With great reluctance, and with dwindling congregations, the building was sold and bought by the venture described above.

At the junction of Charing Cross Road and Shaftesbury Avenue is Cambridge Circus. Here can be seen...

(37) The Palace Theatre.

Built for Richard D'Oyly Carte as the Royal English Opera House to the designs of T E Collcutt and G H Holloway, it opened in 1891 with a romantic opera by Arthur Sullivan, "Ivanhoe". Based on Walter Scott's novel of the same title the opera ran for just one hundred and fifty five performances. In the following year, D'Oyly Carte sold the theatre to August Harris who re-opened it as the Palace Theatre of Varieties. In 1911 the name was changed again, this time to The Palace Theatre - and it has remained such ever since. For the past fifty years it has been "home" to some of the most successful musicals that the West End Theatre has ever known. "Long may it continue to be so".

Cross Charing Cross Road by way of the traffic lights crossing and continue up Charing Cross Road, looking out for the Phoenix Theatre on the right.

(38) The Phoenix Theatre.

Built on the site of a former "place of entertainment" namely the Alcazar described in 1925 as being "a long narrow hall with continuous performances (originally) from noon to midnight". There were three stages and when a performance finished on one the entire audience would walk to the next one - it was standing room only. It was considered by its owners to be a "public audition centre" where talent scouts (who were admitted free) could see the latest musical acts to come to the Metropolis. Unfortunately, the "experiment" did not last long and the site was then used as a "Fun City" with slot-machines, etc. In September 1930 the present building was opened with Noel Coward's "Private Lives". Giles Gilbert Scott, et al., were the architects responsible for the design and Bovis Limited the builders.

Continue in the same direction, a short walk from the theatre, past the various shops of Charing Cross Road, brings the walker back to Tottenham Court Road Underground Station and the start of this walk.

Across the Thames
by Bridge

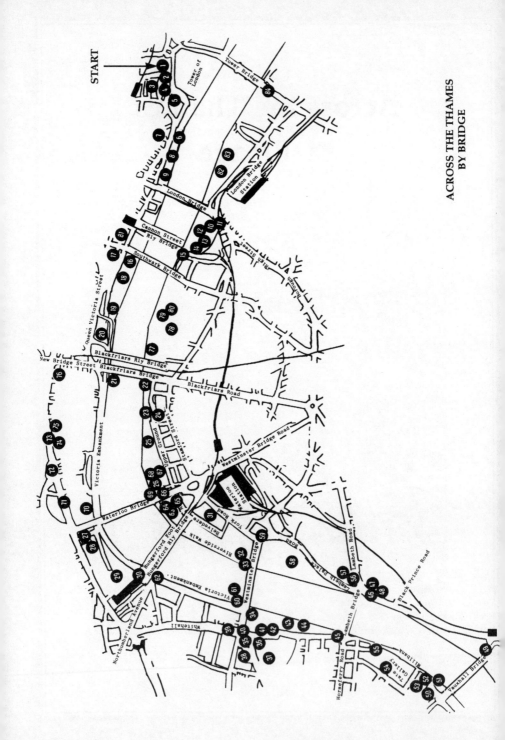

ACROSS THE THAMES
BY BRIDGE

Key to map

1 Tower Hill Underground Station
2 Trinity Square
3 Trinity House
4 Execution Site
5 All Hallows by the Tower Parish Church
6 Customs House
7 St Dunstan in the East church building
8 Former Billingsgate Fish Market
9 St Magnus the Martyr Parish Church
10 Southwark (Anglican) Cathedral
11 Tomb of George Gwilt
12 St Mary Overie's Dock
13 Banqueting House
14 Clink Prison, site of
15 The Anchor Public House
16 Vintners Company Hall
17 St James Garlickhithe Parish Church
18 Queenhithe
19 City of London Boys School
20 Mermaid Theatre
21 Blackfriars Bridge
22 The Doggett's Coat and Badge Public House
23 OXO Building
24 Coin Street Development
25 London Week-end Television Studios and Offices
26 Royal National Theatre
27 Savoy Chapel
28 Savoy Hotel
29 York House Watergate
30 Hungerford Foot Bridge
31 The Shell Centre and Jubilee Gardens
32 The former County Hall for London
33 The Red Lion
34 "Big Ben" clock tower
35 Parliament Square
36 St Margaret Parish Church
37 Westminster Abbey
38 Former Middlesex Guildhall
39 Parliament Street
40 Sir Winston Churchill's statue

41 Oliver Cromwell's statue
42 Richard the Lionheart's statue
43 Victoria Tower
44 Victoria Tower Gardens
45 Lambeth Bridge
46 Albert Embankment
47 International Maritime Organisation
48 London Fire Brigade Headquarters
49 Vauxhall Bridge
50 Morpeth Arms Public House
51 Riverside Gardens
52 "The Dancer"
53 Royal Army Medical College
54 Tate Gallery
55 Millbank Tower
56 Parish Church of St Mary Lambeth
57 Lambeth Palace
58 St Thomas's Hospital
59 Westminster Bridge
60 Queen Boudicea's statue
61 High Tide House
62 Charing Cross Railway Bridge
63 Royal Festival Hall
64 Queen Elizabeth Hall
65 Hayward Gallery
66 National Film Theatre
67 Museum of Moving Image
68 The Royal National Theatre
69 Waterloo Bridge
70 Somerset House
71 Parish Church of St Mary le Strand
72 Parish Church of St Clement Danes
73 Temple Bar Monument
74 Parish Boundary Mark
75 Prince Henry's Room
76 Parish Church of St Bride's Fleet Street
77 Founderers' Arms Public House
78 Bankside Power Station
79 Wren's House
80 New Globe Theatre
81 St Michael Paternoster Royal Church
82 St Olave's House
83 Hay's Galleria
84 Tower Bridge

127

Across The Thames by Bridge

Start: Tower Hill Underground Station.

Circle and District Lines.

Connecting buses: 15, 25, 42, 78

Time: allow approximately 7 hours.

Note: The walk can be divided into several sections if 12 miles is too long to be walked in one go. There are several underground stations on or close to the route at which you can break your exploration. They are Embankment, Pimlico (close to Vauxhall Bridge), Temple and Westminster. Alternatively by using the map one can design their own circular walk joining up the numbered points of interest to suit your requirements.

*O*ne of the most popular nursery rhymes is that which tells the story of London Bridge. "London Bridge is broken down", we sing at our mother's knee, but do we know the significance of what we are singing? 'Once upon a time...' there was only one bridge over the River Thames from its estuary as far up as Tide-end-town (Teddington) and that was the one which connected the Roman City of Londinium with the Royal Burgh of Sudwerche (London Bridge).

It was not until the 18th century that the citizens of Westminster took upon themselves to build a bridge, for which users paid a toll when crossing, in order to reduce travelling time and the delays in crossing London Bridge with its endless traffic queues. The City counteracted the criticisms by building a second bridge themselves - Blackfriars.

Today from Tower Bridge to Richmond Bridge there are eighteen foot and road bridges plus nine railway bridges crossing over the river, and there are plans to build

a new bridge, crossing from Beckton, on the north bank, to Thamesmead in the South. A proposal was recently put before the City of London Corporation to build another new bridge from St Paul's Steps in the City to Bankside, on an axis with the cathedral.

"What is a bridge". A bridge is a way over an impediment whether it be water, chasm, or from one island to another. Bridges can take different forms from the simple log across a countryside stream to a giant cantilever across some major river.

On this walk we shall cross the romantic (Tower Bridge) bridge as well as the slim-line concrete, stone faced bridge (London Bridge). Whatever their construction with whatever material they will all help the walker to cross to the other side of the River Thames.

Starting Point

(1) Tower Hill underground station.

Since a station was first opened in the vicinity in 1882, then called Tower of London, there have been several changes both in name as well as in location for the station which serves Her Majesty's Royal Palace and Fortress of the Tower of London. From 1884 the station was Mark Lane and was across the other side of Trinity Square from the present station. This was re-named in 1946 to become Tower Hill, and was resited to its original place in 1967. In 1988 a new booking hall was constructed which forms the way-in only up to 7pm on a week-day. The exit is through the 1967 booking hall converted to an exit only up to 7pm. In the area beyond the ticket barriers can be seen samples of armour from the Tower of London's collection.

Leave the station by either exit and walk to...

(2) Trinity Square

Named after the "Guild, Fraternity or
Brotherhood of the Most Glorious and
Undivided Trinity", more commonly known as
Trinity House the guardians of the territorial
waters around the coasts of England and
Wales. Their headquarters **(3)** has been here
since 1795, William Pitt the Younger, 1795 -
1806, laid the foundation stone to Samuel
Wyatt"s, 1737 - 1807, design for the building.
Further round the square is the former Port of
London Authority's building, built to the
designs of Sir Edwin Cooper, 1873 - 1942, it
has been described by the late Professor Sir
Nikolaus Pevsner as being "like a super-palace
for an International Exhibition, showy, happily
vulgar and extremely impressive". Whatever
may have been said or written about the
building it did survive an attempt to pull it
down a few years ago after the PLA had moved
'down-stream' to Tilbury with the cessation of
the operations of the docks here.

Continue to walk around the square and
enter into the gardens by way of a gate in
the railings to find...

(4)   Site of the scaffold for public
execution.

The cobble-stoned area is today surrounded by
well-kept flower beds, albeit all blood red in
colour. Here from the nearby Tower of London
prisoners of note were brought and beheaded,
usually watched by a noisy throng of citizens of
London. A "Roll of Dishonour" listing the
more famous (notorious?) names of those
executed here can be seen on the stone mounted
inscriptions around the site. Simon of Sudbury,
Archbishop of Canterbury 1375 - 1381,
together with Sir Robert Hales, the Grand
Prior of the Order of St John of Jerusalem, are
the first two to be listed. They were both
executed on the orders of Wat Tyler the
insurrectionist during the rebellion against the
Poll Tax of the 14th century. Sir Simon Burley,
tutor to Richard II, 1366 - 1399, was the first
official execution', the last one being Simon

Fraser, Lord Lovat in 1747. Lord Lovat failed in
his support of Bonnie Prince Charlie in the
uprising of 1745. He was found guilty having
been captured at Culloden Field and brought to
London, his was the last public beheading in
England. So many people turned up to watch
his execution that a specially erected stand next
to the scaffold collapsed killing several people.
The scaffold was later replaced by a gallows
which claimed its last victims during the
Gordon "No Popery" Riots of the 1780s. They
were a soldier with one arm, and two local
prostitutes who were found guilty of taking
part in a drunken attack on a Roman Catholic
inn-keeper on Tower Hill. From this site can be
seen Sir Edwin Lutyen's, 1869 - 1944,
Mercantile Marine Memorial to the merchant
seamen who died in the First World War, 1914
- 1918. There is also a sunken garden
memorial, by Sir Edward Maufe, for seamen
killed in the Second World War, 1939 - 1945
just behind.

Return to the end of Trinity Square and
cross the roadway to the Parish Church of
All Hallows-by-the-Tower, or
Barkingchurche.

(5)   All Hallows Church.

The church is one of the oldest in the City of
London having been founded in the 7th century
by St Erconwald Bishop of London, 675 - 693,
and given to his sister St Ethelburga, the
Abbess of Barking. Evidence of this early
foundation can be seen in the Saxon Archway
in the west tower of the church. The building
suffered badly in the Second World War, but it
has been well restored in the late Gothic style.
There are many interesting features about the
church and many interesting items to look for
during a visit. In the crypt, open to view with
one of the staff as guide, can be seen a Roman
tesselated pavement, together with a model of
Roman London itself. Also in the crypt is a
stone altar from a Crusader's castle in the Holy
Land. The chapel is a Memorial to members of
the Toc H Movement whose ashes have been

laid to rest here. Behind the cross of the chapel's altar are the ashes of the Rev. "Tubby" Clayton the founder of the Movement which began in an "Upper Room" on the battlefields of the First World War. On the ground floor is the Baptistery with its cover carved by Grinling Gibbons, 1648 - 1721, the wood and stone sculptor who did so much work for Sir Christopher Wren and his rebuilding of the City's churches after the Great Fire of London in 1666. Pause for a moment and look at the painting behind the high altar. It is the "Last Supper" by Brian Thomas, whose works can be seen in a number of other London churches. The eleven Apostles are shown in various poses of prayer and awe, with on the right of the picture, Judas Iscariot disappearing to the High Priests to betray Christ to them. Unusually there are fourteen figures in the painting including a young lad in the right hand corner. This is considered to be John Mark, who as Saint Mark is the author of the fourth Gospel of the New Testament, in whose mother's house the event is said to have taken place. In the North east chapel can be found the Toc H Lamp of Maintenance given to the Movement by the late Duke of Windsor when he was Prince of Wales 1922.

On leaving the church turn left and walk towards Lower Thames Street by the side of the modern office building that has replaced 19th century warehouses, some of which were bombed in the last War, by way of Byward Street. Stop when you come to the Customs' House.

(6)   Customs' House.

The present Custom House was built originally by David Laing, 1774 - 1867, but was partially rebuilt by Sir Robert Smirke, 1781 - 1867, between 1825 and 1826 when the foundations were found to be defective.

To the left hand side of the Custom House is a short roadway that leads down to the river. Here can be viewed the riverside frontage as well as a panoramic view across the river to the south bankside, with HMS Belfast. Return to Lower Thames Street, and turn left. Walk toward London Bridge.

(7)   St Dunstan in the East Church.

Founded in the 13th century, with a list of Rectors going back to 1310, the church was bombed in the Second World War and has been restored as a ruin. Since 1971 when it became an open space of the City it has become a pleasant, green oasis, for the tired walker and the busy office worker to enjoy their lunch in a "garden within a ruined church". The tower and spirelet, designed by Sir Christopher Wren after the Great Fire of London of 1666, has, as he predicted, survived well. First, there was a storm of hurricane force in the early 18th century when nearby houses had the roofs torn off, and then in the 19th and 20th centuries fire destroyed the rest of the church, the tower etc, remained virtually unharmed.

A short distance from the church is...

(8)   Former Billingsgate Fish Market.

After six hundred years the Fish Market moved away from Billingsgate in 1981 to a new home in West India Docks on the Isle of Dogs. From early in the 14th century the Corporation of the City of London was authorised to operate a fish market here at Billingsgate. After the move the building was sold and there was a suggestion to have it demolished, coupled with the prospect that it would collapse once the refrigeration plant in the underground portions were switched off. But, the thaw did not cause the forecast breakdown of the buildings, and it has since been restored by the Richard Rogers architectural practice. With the coming of the 'big bang' in the City it was anticipated that large dealing areas would be needed - but they have not materialised and consequently the building has been "cocooned" at the present time, with an eye to its possible future in the commercial needs of the City of London.

A short distance from the Market and close to London Bridge, is to be found, and visited, if open,

(9) Parish Church of St Magnus the Martyr.

In Richard Newcourt's, "Repertorium", there is mention of the first church on this site in Saxon times being dedicated to St Magnus of Cappadocia who was martyred in 276 at the time of Emperor Aurelian. However in 1924 the official patron of the church was dedicated to be St Magnus the Martyr of Orkney, after a decree issued by the then Bishop of London, the Rt. Rev. Hon. Arthur Foley Winnington-Ingram. Contained in the church today are memorials to a number of famous persons associated with the parish. These include Henry Yevele, c 1320 - 1400, architect of Westminster Hall, once described as the "Wren of the 14th century", Miles Coverdale, 1488 - 1568, one time rector of the parish and the translator of the Holy Bible into English in Geneva between 1557 and 1579. On his death in 1568, he was first buried in the Parish Church of St Bartholomew by the Exchange but that was pulled down in 1841 his remains were translated here. Today the church represents the Anglo-Catholic (High Church) wing of the Church of England and as such has rejuvenated the singing of the Salve Regina after its principle Eucharist on a Sunday morning. For many years the church stood at the foot of Old London Bridge, and when rebuilt after the Great Fire of 1666 allowance had to be made to ensure that the building did not encroach on the approaches to the bridge. With the widening of the bridge in the early 18th century archways were made under the west tower to incorporate the footpath under the tower. On leaving the church find, in the churchyard, stones retained here from the two last London Bridges, while under the tower can be seen a number of parish boundary marks from bygone days.

On leaving the churchyard turn left. Walk along to the flight of stairs under London Bridge which lead to the approaches to the bridge. Keep on the eastern (left hand) side of the bridge.

Walk to the centre of the bridge and admire the view towards Tower Bridge, with HMS Belfast in the mid-foreground. Continue to walk over the bridge, and on the Southwark side cross over the roadway to the flight of steps that lead down to Southwark Cathedral.

(10) Southwark (Anglican) Cathedral

Originally founded as a convent for Benedictine nuns, but when their numbers dropped in the 9th century they were transferred to another convent and replaced by monks of the Augustinian Order.

They remained here until the time of the Dissolution of the Monasteries in the 16th century when the buildings were sold off. The domestic buildings, on the north side of the church, were purchased by the Montagu family who settled there. A group of "Southwark Worthies" bought the church building for the sum of £800, and, after leasing off several parts for secular use, used the remainder of the parish church. In the late 19th century the nave, which had been used by locals as a "free-for-all" stone quarry, was rebuilt to the designs of Sir Arthur Blomfield, 1829 - 1899. With the ever growing population in South London it was decided to raise the church to the dignity of a cathedral and to create a new Anglican diocese of Southwark in 1905. Today the church's full title is "The Collegiate and Cathedral Church of St Saviour and St Mary" and is well-worth a visit. What is the difference between a church and a cathedral? A church is a building set aside, after a solemn consecration service, to the parish and worship of Almighty God. A cathedral is a church in which can be found a "cathedra", ie a bishop's throne. Since the time of the Norman Conquest, 1066 and all that, the Bishops have no authority over the actual cathedral building and the staff. That is the domain of the Dean, or, in the modern cathedrals, a Provost. The change came about at a time when the Bishops were too busy meddling in politics to have time to manage their cathedra as well. So, the senior clergyman, usually a canon or prebendary, was appointed to supervise the running of the cathedral – with the Bishops maintaining their thrones for use when they were invited into the cathedral by the Dean/Provost and Chapter of the cathedral.

After descending the flight of steps leading down from London Bridge note on the right hand side of the tomb **(11)** of George Gwilt, who restored the east end of the cathedral in the 19th century. Also before entering the cathedral by the south west doorway the modern sculpture of "The Holy Family" by Kenneth Hughes just past the south transept. Enter the cathedral by the south west doorway, and explore the building at your leisure.

On leaving the cathedral ascend the short flight of steps to the right and follow the roadway towards…

(12) St Mary Overy Dock.

The enamelled notice at the end of the dock reads that citizens of the Parish of St Saviour's Southwark have the right to unload goods here free from tax. Today the dock houses the Schooner Kathleen & May which has been 'locked-in' by a pair of gates at the river end of the dock. By the riverside is the Old Thameside Public House from which a panoramic view across the river can be enjoyed.

On leaving the inn or from the viewing point to its side, walk forward to the corner of the building and turn right. Immediately can be seen…

(13) Banqueting House of the Bishops of Winchester.

From early days, when Southwark was part of the much larger than today Diocese of Winchester, the bishops maintained a palace here. The ruins are all that remains visible of this most important complex of buildings that the bishops had erected here.

Walk forward leaving the ruins on the left hand side to the corner of Stoney Street. Here on the opposite side of the roadway was the Clink.

(14) Clink Prison, site of.

Deriving from the French word "clenche" meaning a catch or bolt that was attached to the outside of a door making it impossible for any one on the other side to slide it, the anglicised word has become synonymous with "prison". It was a prison for those persons found guilty, or awaiting trial for offences against the Church, The "Clink" has given its name as the slang word for prison. There is now "The Clink Exhibition" on the site.

Walk under the railway bridge which carries the Southern Region trains into Cannon Street Station in the City, noting on the way the blocked in archways that were previously used for railway tracks to bring goods trains into the area for unloading on to carts and deliveries to the nearby warehouses. The wall cranes are still 'in situ' close by.

At the "T" junction turn left where there is…

(15) The Anchor Public House.

Earlier taverns on the site have been shown as being "The Castell upon the Hope", later, at a date unknown, it became "The Anchor on Bankside". The old building was destroyed by fire in 1676, but not before the citizens of London had used it to watch, in dismay, the Great Fire of London in 1666 from its door. In the, then, nearby brewery a special brand of porter was brewed, which was made for the Empress of Russia, it is said to have been Dr Johnson's favourite drink. The tales of the inn are multiple with the river pirates and the Press Men taking pride of place among them. The pirates would enter the bar of the house, demand payment for their ill-gotten gains - brandy on which neither tax nor toll had been paid - receive like for like, drink it, and then disappear again to rob another ship lying in the Pool of London. If danger threatened then they would "nod and wink" at the bar staff and be allowed into the private quarters of the house. Here they would hide in a 'cupboard' into which a secret doorway had been built that led into a shaft in the centre of the building. Here they would be safe until danger had passed. The Press Gangs took no such evasive action they would descend on the house and quickly, quietly, remove any fit and healthy man that they could find. Perhaps with a quick "tap" on the head, the recipient of which would be likely to wake up some time later and discover that he had "enlisted" in the Royal Navy for a tour off duty. The gangs did not take all their victims from the taverns but sometimes acted "under orders". There is the delightful story of how, one day, while crossing the river by ferry, Samuel Pepys, 1633 - 1703, the famous 17th century Diarist and Secretary to the Navy Office, was overcharged by a farthing for the journey. Shortly afterwards the ferry man found he too had joined the Navy! Today the area around the house has been pedestrianised with a terrace by the riverside from which vantage point the City may be viewed and the river watched as it passes by "The Anchor on Bankside".

Continue to walk along the riverside promenade until Southwark Bridge is reached ascend the steps to the bridge. Cross over the roadway and walk along the left hand side of the bridge towards the City. Pause for a moment in the centre and admire the view towards Blackfriars road and railway bridges.

Queen Street Place is at the northern end of the bridge. At the junction with Upper Thames Street turn left. Here is…

(16) Vintners' Hall

The Worshipful Company of Vintners of the City of London are 11th in Order of Precedence of the Livery Companies and were first recognised as a guild in July 1346 when they were granted the monopoly of all the wine trade of Gascony. Their first Hall was destroyed in the Great Fire of 1666, and was replaced by the present building two years later. The front of the building, being part of a later restoration has a pair of fine wrought iron gates to the main entrance. On the gates can be seen swans reminding the passer-by that, together with the Dyers' Company, the Vintners take part in the Swan-Upping ceremony each year. At this time the two Companies mark (nick) a number of the young cygnets on the river while leaving the rest for the Queen. All swans on the river are the property of the reigning Monarch, but these two companies have the privilege to 'own' a certain number marking them with, for the Dyers' one nick on the beak, and for the Vintners two. Many inns owned by the Vintners' Company were called the "Swan with two nicks", later translated as being the "Swan with two necks". Note the swans on the gateways once again. In 1363 the Company entertained five kings to dinner viz. the Kind of England, Edward III, David of Scotland, John of France, and the kings of Cyprus and Denmark. When the Master of the Company is toasted, in wine! it is followed by Five Cheers instead of the customary three, "thus perpetuating the memory of the Feast of Five Kings in 1363", so writes the author of "A brief story of the Worshipful Company of Vintners".

Across the roadway from the hall stands…

(17) St James Garlickhithe Parish Church.

There has been a church on this site since Saxon times, with a 'first mention' in the record books dating from 1196. The same book shows that in 1326 Sheriff Richard Rothing had the church rebuilt at his own expense. This building was destroyed in the Great Fire of 1666 and was rebuilt by Sir Christopher Wren. In 1876 the nearby church of St Michael's

Queenhithe was pulled down and some of the internal fittings were transferred to St James' among which were the pulpit, choir stalls and a lion and unicorn. It was while fitting in the new stalls for the choir that a mummified body of a man was discovered under the old stalls. Who he was nobody knows. Today he 'lives' in a room in the tower, and is rarely shown to visitors. There is a tradition in the parish that 'once upon a time' the choirboys would give him an airing and dance him around the church. There are no choirboys to continue the practice today. Neither are there any children to perpetuate the old custom of making a "St James' Grotto" on the saint's feastday, 25th July. In pre-Second World War days, the children of London would make their grottos on the pavements near their homes and ask for "A penny for the Grotto". What they did with the money I do not know! In July 1988 the Rector, Rev. John Paul, rededicated the magnificent 17th century clock over the west doorway to the church. It had been knocked down during the Blitz of 1940 - 41 from its bracket and its restoration was the brain-child of Mr Michael Fairbank a Past Master of the Vintners' Company. It is to this church that the Vintners Company process each year after the election of the new Master. In font of the procession there are two, white-smocked, wine porters who sweep the way clear for the Master, Wardens, Beadle and members of the Court of Assistants of the Company. The Master and his retinue carry posies of sweet smelling herbs and flowers to keep away the "smells of the streets".

Return to the other side of the roadway and walk away from the Vintners' Place. Walk on past Bull Wharf Lane to…

(18) Queenhithe

At the end of the lane is one of the oldest of the docks of the City of London - Queenhithe. A 'hithe' is an "inlet" in the bank of a river at which goods are unloaded, the 'queen' here being Queen Matilda, wife of Henry I, 1068-1135. Later Queens of England inherited the hithe and received an income in the form of a percentage of the taxes paid by the boatmen. Once again there is a panoramic view across the river with the Bankside Power Station dominating the south bank skyline, to the left of which can be seen the houses of the Provost and Sacrist of Southwark Cathedral and the house next door where Sir Christopher Wren lived for a time.

Return to Upper Thames Street. Turn left. Shortly will be seen a small lane that leads down to the riverside walk. Here is …

(19) City of London Boys' School.

Founded in the 15th century under the will of the Town Clerk, John Carpenter, moved to its present site in 1986, from a building on the Victoria Embankment near Blackfriars' Bridge. To say that Carpenter actually founded the school is really a slight misnomer, it was the accumulating of the money that he had left to educate "four boys born within the City of London" who became known as "Carpenters' Boys". By the 19th century, the money had accrued sufficiently for the Corporation to petition Parliament to allow them to build a boys' school in the City.

Continue to walk along the riverside wall to the…

(20) Mermaid Theatre

The inspiration of Lord Miles of Blackfriars (Bernard Miles, the actor-manager) and his wife, the theatre was formally opened by the Lord Mayor of London, Sir Harold Gillet, 28th May 1959 when "the bells of St Paul's Cathedral pealed out a welcome as the doors of the theatre opened for the first "first night" in the City since the Lord Mayors of the Elizabethan age drove actors from the City as "rogues and vagabonds". The auditorium has been built out of the ruins of a 19th century warehouse that had been bombed during the Second World War. It has a single-tiered interior designed on the lines of a Greek amphitheatre, with 500 seats all with a direct view of the stage. The first production "Lock up your daughters" was an immediate success. In later years the whole of the complex was rebuilt with the theatre of today being incorporated into an office building.

Walk forward to the flight of steps which lead up to…

(21) Blackfriars Bridge

This was the third bridge to be built over the river and was opened to traffic in 1769. It was first named the "Pitt Bridge", after the Earl of Chatham, William Pitt the Elder, 1708-1778, and the foundation stone is now in the care of the Museum of London. When the original bridge was replaced in 1865, a new foundation stone was laid by Queen Victoria, 1819-1901, at which time the bridge was renamed the "Blackfriars". From one of the abutments, lovingly called 'pulpits' from their design, can be seen the stone pillars that once supported the railway lines from Blackfriars railway station. The rails and the bridge have been removed but the columns remain - doubtless these will confuse future archaeologists who may consider them to be a 19th century Stonehenge of the River Thames!

Walk across the bridge once again crossing the Thames, keeping to the left hand side, and at the other side cross over the roadway and walk back towards the bridge. Here can be seen…

(22) Doggett's Coat and Badge public house.

It is highly appropriate that a place of refreshment bearing this name should be by the riverside. An Irish comedian by the name of Thomas Doggett came to live in London in the late 17th century. He left money in his will to commemorate the accession to the Throne of England of George I, 1660 - 1717, for a rowing

race to be held annually from Chelsea to London Bridge towards the end of July. The winner receives a scarlet coat and a silver badge.

Retrace the route to Upper Ground. Walking along Upper Ground look out for the former OXO building (23) with the name in the brick window of the tower and on the opposite side of the roadway the Coin Street Development (24). Also the London Week-end Television building (LWT) (25), followed shortly afterwards by the Royal National Theatre (26).

(26) The Royal National Theatre.

The theatre was designed by Sir Denis Lasdun, b. 1914. The construction of the theatre took place between 1969 and 1976, and it was officially opened by HM the Queen in 1977. The opening was the culmination of much hard work, and on many occasions, controversy. The idea for a National Theatre was first proposed in 1848, but it was not until 1949 that the National Theatre Bill allowed for the sum of £1,000,000 and the setting up of a Commission to consider the building of the theatre. The Queen, while still HRH the Princess Elizabeth, in 1951 laid the foundation stone during the Festival of Britain on behalf of her father George VI, 1895-1952, Lord Chandos in 1962 accepted the chairmanship of the National Theatre Board, with Sir Lawrence (later Lord) Olivier as the Artistic Director. In the run-up to the completion of the building the National Theatre Company took over the Old Vic Theatre in Waterloo Road. The Company moved into their new premises in 1976.

Follow the signs that direct one to Waterloo Bridge. Cross the bridge on the left hand side admiring the view towards "Big Ben" and the former home of the Greater London Council - County Hall.

The approach roadway to the northern side of the bridge is Lancaster Place. At the Strand turn left, and left again down Savoy Ward street.

(27) Savoy Chapel

The chapel is all that is left above ground of the former Savoy Palace that was built for Peter, Earl of Savoy and Richmond. During the time of the Wat Tyler rebellion in 1381 over the Poll Tax the palace was destroyed, and rebuilt. In 1450 another rebel Jack Cade, after lynching a number of unpopular officials in London, ransacked the palace before dispersing and returning to his native Kent. On this occasion when the palace was rebuilt it became a hospital for one hundred poor men, and a new chapel (church) was built. This building survives and serves as the "Chapel Royal of the Royal Victorian Order" by Royal Decree of HM King George VI. The chapel has played an important part in the development of the Church of England since the time of the English Reformation in the 16th century. It was hot to the Savoy Conference of 1661 that produced the revised edition of the Book of Common Prayer. Ronnie Ellen in his excellent book "A London Steeplechase", published in 1972, but now, alas, out of print, states "It resulted in the still-statutory Prayer Book of 1661" - a point that is strongly defended by the Prayer Book Society. "Members of the public are most welcome to attend all the Services here notified", says the weekly service sheet. It makes a pleasant oasis in the hustle and bustle of the modern city 'just up the hill'.

Walk down Savoy Hill to Savoy Place. Turn right. Shortly will be seen…

(28) Savoy Hotel, riverside entrance.

The success of the D'Oyly Carte Company in presenting the operettas of Gilbert and Sullivan in the Savoy Theatre that had been specially built for them by Richard D'Oyly Carte in 1881 prompted him to build a hotel next to the theatre. The hotel was designed by Thomas Edward Colcutt, 1840 - 1924, and financed by Richard D'Oyly Carte. It was opened in 1889, since when there have been a number of additions and alterations to the original building. The Strand approach road to the main entrance to the building is the only roadway in Britain where vehicles must keep to the right-hand side of the road.

Continue along Savoy Place, at the end of which the roadway 'disappears' under the building. Follow it round, being careful of the cars that use it as a quick, jam-free, approach to the Victoria Embankment. This is Lower Robert Street, and leads to Robert Street in the Adelphi. Turn left at the junction with John Adam Street. Walk along to Buckingham Street and turn left. Note on the right-hand side of the roadway the plaque commemorating Samuel Pepys's residence here. At the end of the street there are some steps which lead down to Watergate. Here can be seen…

(29) York House, Watergate.

Standing on its original site the Watergate was the 17th century entrance to the grounds of York House. The house was one of a number of residences of the Archbishops of York, and was acquired by Archbishop Heath in the reign of Queen Mary, 1553 - 1558, for the use of himself and his successors. In the reign of James I, 1603 - 1625, it became the property of the Crown. When George Villiers, Duke of Buckingham, 1592 - 1628, obtained the house he pulled down York House and rebuilt it. The Watergate is the only part of his structure left today. It was designed by Inigo Jones, 1573 - 1652, and the work was carried out by Nicholas Stone, in 1626. In the library of Sir John Soane, in Lincoln's Inn Fields, there is the "Account book of workes by Nicholas Stone" which records… "ye right hand lion hee did, fronting ye Thames. Mr Kearne, a Jarman, his brother marrying, did ye shee lion". All the stone came from the stone quarries being used for the restoration of St Paul's Cathedral at that time. On the riverside are the arms of the Villiers family, and on the reverse side can be seen their family motto - Fidei Coticula Crux (The Cross is the Touchstone of Faith).

At the foot of the steps turn right and walk along to another short flight of steps which lead to Villiers Street. Turn left. Walk down the Embankment underground station, through the booking hall, to the Embankment. On the right is a flight of steps which lead up to...

(30) Hungerford Footbridge, alongside the Charing Cross railway bridge.

The previous bridge, also for foot passengers only, was built by Brunel between 1841 - 1845 and was a suspension bridge. When the present railway bridge that runs alongside the foot-bridge was built in 1863 from the designs of F Brady, the old bridge's suspension cables were re-used for the Clifton Suspension Bridge in Bristol, where they still support one of the finest bridges of its kind, and class, in the world.

When walking across the foot-bridge stop occasionally to admire the view towards the City of London, as well as the modern developments of the South Bank complex. Leave the bridge by way of the stairs that lead to the Riverside Walk. Immediately under the bridge, on the left hand side can be seen...

(31) The Shell Centre & Jubilee Gardens.

The giant office block belonging to the international petroleum and chemicals company Shell was built to Sir Howard Robertson's designs between 1957 and 1962. It covers a seven and a half acre site, and was the largest office building in Europe at the time of its completion. About 5,000 people work at the Centre who were gathered in from thirty different buildings from all over London in the early 1960s. At the top of the twenty-five storey building there is a viewing gallery which, unfortunately, is not open to members of the public.

In front of the Shell Centre are the Jubilee Gardens that were laid out on part of the land acquired at the time of the Festival of Britain in 1951. Note the lamp-standards along the riverside that are exact copies of those erected on the north bank during the time of the construction of the Victoria Embankment in the 19th century, only the date and the monogram of the reigning monarch are different.

Walk towards the next bridge (Westminster Bridge) just before which can be seen...

(32) County Hall.

This was the home for the London County Council, for whom it was built in the earlier part of this century, and for its successor the Greater London Council. The latter was dissolved in 1986, a fact noted on a plaque outside the former main entrance to the building, having taken over from the LCC in 1965. The building was designed by Ralph Knott with the construction work being under the direct supervision of the Council's chief engineer Sir Maurice Fitzmaurice, and his successor Sir Geo. Humphrays. The two World Wars of this century interrupted the completion of the buildings and it was not until 1963 that the last, and final, block of the complex was opened. In 1995 the future of the buildings is still being debated(?).

Walk up the stairs at the end of the Riverside Walk. Here can be found...

(33) The "Red" Lion.

The full size lion is made of Coade Stone and was once on the roof line of the Red Lion Brewery which stood next to Hungerford Bridge. When the brewery was pulled down at the time that South Bank was being prepared for the Festival of Britain in 1951, the lion was 'lost', only to re-appear at the time of the Festival on a plinth on the corner of the entrance roadway to Waterloo Station. It was re-erected here in 1966, weighing 13 tons, it stands 12ft high and acts as guardian to both the bridge and Parliament on the other side of the river.

Cross the bridge (Westminster) noting on the way the various coats of arms which have been used to decorate it.

Here are the arms of Queen Victoria, Prince Albert, Edward, Prince of Wales (later Edward VII), together with those of Sir William Molesworth, 1st Commissioner Board of Works, 1853, and Henry John Temple Palmerston, Prime Minister, 1855-1858, 1859 - 1865.

On the other side of the bridge, cross the roadways either by using the traffic lights' crossing, or by descending the steps which lead to the embankment of Westminster pier and by using the subway. Exit by the tunnel which leads to the Houses of Parliament and Parliament Square.

On the western side of Westminster Bridge stands the Royal Palace of Saint Stephen at Westminster, commonly called the "Houses of Parliament".

Rising 320ft above ground level is...

(34) "Big Ben", more correctly St Stephen's Clocktower.

One of the best known of the sights of London the clock tower houses that most famous of bells - "Big Ben" - weighing thirteen and a half

tons, it is said to take its name from the First Commissioner of Works, Sir Benjamin Hall. Hansard, the official diary of the proceedings of the Houses of Parliament, records that during a debate as to what to call the tower, it had been suggested simply "St Stephen's", and that the giant bell on which the hours were to be struck "St Stephen's Bell". The debate was long and arduous until one restive back bencher called out "Why not call it "Big Ben" and be done with it?". This was the House's nick-name for the Commissioner of Works, the name was duly settled amid laughter from all sides of the house and so it has remained ever since.

Look up, on the Parliament Square side of the tower and there, under the clock-face can be seen inscribed "Victoria prima". The Queen was determined that the world should know that she was the first of a possible long line of Victorias to follow.

(35) Parliament Square.

The square that was laid out as part of the 'new' Houses of Parliament in the 19th century, was re-arranged in 1951 to its present layout. Around the square can be seen the Parish Church of both Westminster and the Houses of Parliament, St Margaret's (36). Behind it is Westminster Abbey (37), and directly opposite, Parliament the former Middlesex Guildhall (38). On the eastern side Parliament Street (39) leads into Whitehall. Around the square there are a number of statues of prominent parliamentarians. The one nearest to the former royal palace is Sir Winston Churchill (40).

A diversion around the square and a visit to the church and abbey might be considered. After which, or instead of, the walk continues along the outside of the Houses of Parliament towards Lambeth Bridge (45). On the way can be seen...

(41) Statue of Oliver Cromwell, 1599 - 1658.

The work of Sir William Hamo Thornycroft, 1850 - 1925, it succeeds in conveying both the sense of piety (with a Bible in his hand) and power (with the sword in the other hand). When it was first erected there were a number of protests from the supporters of Charles I, 1600 - 1649, who considered that Cromwell was the chief perpetrator of the King's death. Immediately behind the statue is Westminster Hall, one of the few remaining portions of the medieval palace that was not destroyed in the fire of 1834. It was once used as the Royal Courts of Justice and was the setting for many great trials including that of Charles I and Guy Fawkes.

(42) Statue of Richard the Lionheart, 1157 - 1199.

Baron Carlo Marochetti, 1805 - 1867, an Italian sculptor settled in London in 1848, and was commissioned to produce a statue of Richard I. It was erected in 1860 in front of the 'new' House of Lords, as part of Barry's overall design for the area following the fire of 1834. During the Second World War the king's sword was damaged by the blast from a bomb that fell nearby. At first it was agreed that it should remain as an act of defiance to all who dared invade England. However, after the severe winter of 1947 it was decided that the sword was a hazard to the public and it was subsequently restored.

On the opposite side of the roadway stands the statue of George V, 1865 - 1936, by Sir William Reid Dick, 1879 - 1961. At the western end of the Houses of Parliament is the...

(43) Victoria Tower

Standing 336ft high and 75ft square, the tower houses the archives of Parliament, which include the voting papers from the last General Election. On the Eve of a General Election the papers are removed and burnt away from the Houses of Parliament for fear of another disastrous fire like the one which destroyed the previous buildings in the last century.

Walk past the Victoria Tower and enter into...

(44) Victoria Tower Gardens.

This pleasant triangular shaped open space makes a welcome respite from the hard paving stones of the city's walkways. Just inside the entrance there is a statue to Mrs Emmeline Pankhurst, 1858-1928, the suffragette, by Thomas Woolner, 1825 - 1892. **(45).** Beyond the statue can be seen a copy of the "Burghers of Calais" by Auguste Rodin, 1840 - 1917, **(46),** the original stands in the town square in Calais. To commemorate the emancipation of

slavery in the former British Empire, (now called the Commonwealth of Nations), there was erected in the north west corner of Parliament Square a drinking fountain, coupled with the name of Sir Thomas Fowell Buxton, a Member of Parliament, and well-known social reformer of the 19th century. It was designed by his son, Charles Buxton. Octagonal in shape it is polished, pink, granite, grey stone and white marble. On the corners are bronze statuettes of British rulers from Caratacus to Queen Victoria. It was moved in after the 1951 re-arrangements in Parliament Square. At the far end of the gardens there is a children's playground.

Walk up the steps at the end of the garden to the approaches to...

(45) Lambeth Bridge

Between the two banks of the River Thames here there was a ferry, a floating platform that was capable of transporting not only people but horses and carriages. Hence the approach roadway to the bridge on the northern side being called Horseferry Road. The ferry was run on behalf of the Archbishop of Canterbury whose rights to the fees from it dated back to "time out of memory" as John Stow, 1525-1605 would have said. When the first bridge was erected over the river here, the Archbishop, the Rt. Rev. Charles Thomas Longley, 1794 - 1868, received the sum of £2,200 for "loss of income". The bridge opened in 1862, was a suspension construction and lasted until 1929 when it was pulled down and replaced in 1932 by the present one. The use of pineapples to decorate the bridge recall the fact that the fruit was first introduced into this country in the 17th century by the Tradescant family.

Pause on the bridge and admire the view towards the Houses of Parliament. At the foot of the bridge cross over the roadway and walk along...

(46) Albert Embankment

Until the latter part of the 19th century much of the south bank of the river here was subject to flooding from high tides, and it was not until the building of the embankment by Sir Joseph Bazalgette, 1819 - 1891, between 1866 and 1870, that extensive building work took place. The area had been used by boat-builders, who had as their neighbours, the Lambeth Pottery works that were first established here in the 16th century. Today the buildings along the embankment are all modern in construction one of which contains the International Maritime Organisation. **(47).** Designed by Douglas Marriot, Worby and Robinson practice of architects, it won the Worshipful Company of Carpenters' Award for 1981-1982. The IMO is an agency of the United Nations that is concerned with safety at sea, and the prevention of sea pollution. HM the Queen formally opened the building in 1983. Next to the IMO is the London Fire Brigade's Headquarters **(48)**, designed by architects of the LCC and opened by George VI, 1895 - 1952, in 1937, just in time to cope with the many fires of the Second World War, 1939 - 1945. This is the central control for all fires in the London area. The pier opposite the building is the river base for Firebrace the appliance used at fires that have the river as one of their boundaries, or should there be a fire aboard one of the shops on the river.

Continue to walk along Albert Embankment, noting the modern buildings on both sides of the river. The roadway and footpath leave the riverside opposite Inworth Street, and then it is a short walk to the southern approaches of...

(49) Vauxhall Bridge.

In 1811 Lord Dundas laid the foundation stone here for what was to become the first of a number of new bridges that were built over the river in the 19th century. The bridge was first called Regent's Bridge but soon after it was opened in 1816 by the Prince Regent, later George IV, 1762 - 1830, it was re-named Vauxhall. It connected two important areas of development of the 19th century. The bridge, rebuilt between 1902 - 1906, has a number of interesting features which include eight bronze statues that represent the Arts and Sciences. Facing upstream are Engineering, Architecture, while looking downstream are Fine Arts, Local Government, Science and Education. With the lowering in recent years the balustrade of the bridge they are more easily seen, but care should be taken not to topple over into the river below!

After crossing the bridge turn right from the right hand side and walk back towards Lambeth Bridge (45) along Millbank. Almost immediately there is, once again, a pleasant oasis in which to rest awhile. On the opposite side of the roadway is the...

(50) Morpeth Arms Public House.

This 19th century building stands close to where the Millbank Penitentiary was opened in 1821 and there are still stories told of the underground tunnel that linked where now the public house stands to the prison and how prisoners were sometimes able to escape through it. Today's host has provided benches and chairs for his clientele who are asked to leave quietly in consideration of the residential nature of the area today.

(51) Riverside Gardens

Here can be seen "Locking Piece" by Henry Moore, 1898 - 1968, which is said to have been inspired by his finding two stones fitted together while strolling through his garden. At the other end of the gardens is a bollard that was used to tie the barges to which were to take the prisoners from the penitentiary down-stream to the larger ships conveying them to Australia and New Zealand as punishment for their crimes. An inscription on the bollard notes its historical importance.

Continue along Millbank.

(52) "The Dancer".

On the last house of the terrace of houses that fronts the river along Millbank is the statue "Jette", by Enzo Plazzotta, which is based on the dancer David Wall, 1946 —. Next to the statue is the Officers Mess of the Royal Army Medical Corps.

(53) Royal Army Medical College.

Founded in 1860 at Chatham, and after a short stay at Netley in Hampshire, it came here in 1907 to a building designed by Wood & Ainslie. The College provides post-graduate studies in military surgery, etc. and is on part of the site of the Millbank Penitentiary. In the courtyard to the side of the building is the statue by Matthew Noble, 1817 - 1876, of Sir James McGrigor, 1771 - 1858, who was virtually the Founder of the RAMC. Originally the statue was erected in the grounds of the Royal Hospital, Chelsea but moved here in 1909.

Across Atterbury Street from the college is…

(54) Tate Gallery.

Built on another part of the penitentiary site, the Gallery, designed by Sidney Smith, was built with funds provided by Sir Henry Tate, 1819 - 1899, the sugar refiner who patented a method of cutting sugar loaves into cubes. He presented the Gallery together with a collection of his pictures to the nation in 1897. Since its foundation there have been a number of extensions added to the original building which include one by Sir Joseph Duveen for the Turner Collection, and his son paid for a further extension to house modern foreign paintings. The Gallery also has a fine collection of paintings of William Blake, 1757 - 1827. In 1987 the Clore extension was opened to house the enlarged William Turner Collection. No visit to the Gallery is complete without eating or drinking in the restaurant whose walls are decorated with Rex Whistler's drawings of the

"Pursuit of Rare Meats". In the gardens surrounding the building are examples of the work of Henry Moore and Barbara Hepworth.

Continue to walk along the riverside and on the left can be seen...

(55) Millbank Tower

Built for the Vickers Group between 1960 - 1963 to the designs of Ronald Ward & Partners, the tower block rises 387ft, and was one of the earliest office tower blocks to be built in the 1960s.

From the Tower it is a short walk to Lambeth Bridge (45). Walk over the bridge and turn left - here are side by side an archbishop's palace and a former parish church.

(56) Parish Church of St Mary at Lambeth.

On 31st October 1972 the last service was held here, after which the whole congregation processed to the local Methodist Church whose premises they now share. After hundreds of years of witness to the Christian Faith the church was declared redundant. All that is left of the medieval church is the 14th century west tower, the remainder of the building having been rebuilt in 1851 to the designs of Philip Hardwick, 1792 - 1870. Today the church houses the Museum of Garden History, and is in the care of the Tradescant Trust that was set up in 1977. This would seem to be an appropriate organisation to both run a museum of this nature and to be coupled with the name of the Tradescants. Two John Tradescants, father and son, were gardeners to Charles I and his Queen, Henrietta Maria, and were responsible for introducing into this country such flowers as the "Michaelmas Daisy", "Stocks", "Jasmine", as well as the popular plant that bears their name - "Tradescantias". Their tomb is in the churchyard alongside that of Admiral Bligh of the "Bounty". Part of the

churchyard has now been fenced off and is planted with plants which they introduced, as well as others contemporary to their time.

(57) Lambeth Palace.

The London home of His Grace the Archbishop of Canterbury since the time that Archbishop Hubert Walter, 1193 - 1207, and the Bishop of Rochester, Gilbert de Glanvil, 1185 - 1214, arranged an exchange of houses between themselves. At this time the house consisted of a Manor House, and it was not until the time of Archbishop Boniface, 1245 - 1273, that the present complex was erected, with the permission of the Pope, Urban IV, 1261 - 1264. From time to time since there have been additions to the buildings within the confines of the wall surrounding the Palace. In 1648 the palace and grounds were confiscated and a Commonwealth Garrison was stationed there. Horses were to be found in the Great Hall, and in other parts Royalists, supporters of Charles I, were imprisoned. At the Restoration of the Monarchy in 1660 Archbishop William Juxon, 1660 - 1663, set about rebuilding the ruins. The Gatehouse was built in the 15th century at the instigation of Archbishop John Morton, 1486 - 1501, in the following century Archbishop Thomas Cranmer, 1533 - 1556, declared various judgements on the validity, or otherwise, on the marriage of Henry VIII, 1491 - 1547, to Anne Boleyn. Both Mary Tudor and her step-sister Elizabeth I, 1533 - 1603 were constant visitors to the Palace for "advice and comfort". The Palace is open to members of the public from time to time, and private parties are allowed but first, write to The Secretary at the Palace.

The gardens of the palace are also open to the public from time to time, and are well worth a visit. In recent years, under the skilful hands of Mrs Rosalind Runcie, wife of the former Archbishop of Canterbury, they were transformed from a lawn setting into one, which contains among other attractions, a herb garden, cottage and Chinese gardens, with a wild woodland garden at the end of the path which circumnavigates the garden. Beyond the walled garden of the palace is "Archbishop's Park" that once formed part of the palace's ground which in the 19th century, was transferred on perpetual loan to the local authority.

Walk along the riverside wall of the palace, to reach Archbishop's Park on the right hand side of the roadway. At the appropriate place cross over, by where the traffic lights are, to…

(58) St Thomas's Hospital.

Founded originally in Southwark as part of the Priory of Mary Overie in the 12th century, it moved to this site in 1871 when it was opened by Queen Victoria, 1819 - 1901. The hospital's history is bound up with that of Florence Nightingale who founded a training school for nurses at the hospital. In 1989 the Florence Nightingale Museum was opened at the hospital as a further tribute to the "Grand Old Lady of the Crimean War".

Walk along the pavement by the hospital until the approach road to Westminster Bridge (59).

(59) Westminster Bridge.

The original bridge was opened in 1750 with money that had been raised from a national lottery, the winning tickets being drawn in the Jerusalem Chamber of Westminster Abbey. In 1862 it was discovered that the bridge's foundations had become insecure, due to the vast increase of traffic that passed over it daily, and a new, the present, bridge was built. Designed by Thomas Page it consists of seven iron arches, and is a notably wide bridge being 84ft across, this enabled trams from 1906 to 1953 to use one side of the roadway without interfering with the rest of the traffic. The length of the bridge is 811ft and 6 inches, and has often been used as a 'race against time' track with runners trying to run across the bridge before "Big Ben" has finished chiming twelve o'clock - not all have succeeded!

Cross the bridge for the 2nd time walking along on the left hand side until the Westminster side. Here cross the roadway (right), using the traffic light crossing. On reaching the other side of the roadway. Pause and look up at…

(60) Statue of Queen Boudicea.

The Queen was the widow of Prasutagus, King of the Iceni tribe in East Anglia during the 1st century, on whose death, the Roman Procurator seized all his possessions, in spite of the fact that the king had left half his property to the Romans and half to his wife. The Queen protested!! A general revolt followed during which time the Queen 'laid-flat' Colchester, Verulamium (St Alban's) and finally London. In a great battle, possibly near where King's Cross Station stands today, the Iceni tribesmen were routed and the Queen took poison rather than surrender to the Romans. The statue was the work of Thomas Thornycroft, 1815 - 1885, and shows the Queen with her two daughters in a Roman styled chariot with galloping horses, with no one apparently driving and without a harness. From the hubs of the wheels there are scythes. It was erected in 1902.

Descend the steps on the right hand side of the statue to the riverside walk by Westminster Pier. At the foot of the steps on the right hand side is…

(61) High Tide House.

This is an open column, the inside of which is marked in the form of a measure that enables the height of the tides at Westminster Bridge to be recorded. This is followed shortly afterwards by the pier from which pleasure cruises on the river depart. Across the river can be seen the former County Hall of London.

Walk past the pier along Victoria Embankment towards Hungerford Foot & the Charing Cross Railway Bridges.

(62) Charing Cross Railway Bridge or Hungerford Bridge.

The bridge, on the site of the former Hungerford Suspension Bridge, was built for the South Eastern Railway Company, which is now part of the Southern Regions of British Rail, from the designs of Sir John Hawkshaw. It was started in 1860 and completed three years later, in 1882 the bridge was widened under the direction of F Brady. On the other side of the railway bridge is the Hungerford Foot Bridge that can be reached by way of steps to the side of the Embankment Underground Station.

Walk across the bridge, admiring once more the view towards the City of London with St Paul's Cathedral dominating the skyline which it shares with the tall office blocks of the City. At the end of the bridge descend to the riverside walk in front of...

(63) Royal Festival Hall.

Built as part of the Festival of Britain in 1951 it has become an integrated part of the South Bank Arts Complex. Designed by Sir Leslie Martin, and extended by Sir Hubert Bennett, both being Architects to the London County Council, the hall is a favourite rendezvous for musicians both classical and popular. Close by is the Queen Elizabeth Hall, and the Hayward Gallery - opened in 1967/68 they too are the work of Sir Hubert Bennett and his team of architects of London County Council. (64/65)

Pass under Waterloo Bridge **(69)** with the National Film Theatre **(66)** nestling under its arches, with the Museum of Moving Image a close companion **(67)**. on the 'other side of the bridge' is...

(68) The Royal National Theatre.

After many years of debate the Theatre finally was built here and opened for its first performances in 1977. The architect for the building, "liked by some and hated by others", was Sir Denys Lasdun.

From the Royal National Theatre find the steps which lead to...

(69) Waterloo Bridge.

The first Waterloo Bridge was the result of the setting up of the Strand Bridge Company in the early 19th century. It resulted in John Rennie, 1761 - 1821, being appointed to design the bridge. The Prince Regent, later George IV, opened the bridge 18th June 1817, by which time the name had been changed from Strand to Waterloo. Italian sculptor Antonio Canova, 1757-1822, hailed the bridge as being "the noblest bridge in the world... alone worth come to London to see". However, with the increase of traffic, the wear and tear on the bridge caused it to sag and by 1925 a temporary bridge was erected by its side. When the proposals to demolish Rennie's bridge and to replace it were made public, there was an outcry. The Leader of the London County Council at that time was Herbert Morrison who said on one occasion "We need a modern artery and not an ancient monument to serve London". Work on the new bridge was begun in 1937, and was partially opened to traffic five years later. It was formally opened in 1944, at which time the temporary bridge was carefully dismantled and re-used to bridge the River Rhine in Germany as part of the advancing Allied offensive during the latter part of the Second World War. Today's bridge was designed by Sir Giles Gilbert Scott, 1880 - 1960, and was the first bridge across the

Thames to be built of reinforced concrete it is "a continuous girder with cantilevers and suspended span construction". The former bridge was made of granite that was later used to form part of the foundations of the M3 motorway - so the bridge continues to serve the traffic.

Walk over the bridge on the right-hand side. Pause to admire the view towards the City of London. At the northern end is Lancaster Place and…

(70) Somerset House

The site on which Somerset House stands has a long and interesting history. In medieval times the chapel of the Holy Innocents stood here, and later became the first Parish Church of St Mary Le Strand. The church was pulled down by the Protector Somerset, Edward Seymour, Earl of Hertford and Duke of Somerset, 1506 - 1552, who as the uncle of Edward VI, 1537 - 1553, obtained the post of Protector to the young king. In its place the Protector had built a house for himself - Somerset House - with much of the stone coming from monastic buildings in and around London. Not even the Great Cloister of St Paul's Cathedral was exempt from his pillaging, more stone coming from St John's Priory in Clerkenwell, and the houses of the Bishops of Chester and Worcester. There is a story that he parleyed with the monks of Westminster to spare destruction of their Abbey in exchange for the stones of St Martin Le Grand in the City of London, which was their daughter house. After his beheading in 1552, the land and house passed into the hands of the Crown. In the 17th century the house and grounds became an unexpected centre for members of the Roman Catholic Church, when Queens Henrietta Maria (wife of Charles I) and Catherine Braganza (wife of Charles II) took up residence here. Inigo Jones, 1573 - 1652, himself a Catholic was commissioned to design a chapel for the house. When the present house was built between 1776 and 1786, to the designs of Sir William

Chambers, 1723 - 1796, the tombs of various attendants of the two Queens were found in the cellars underneath the present courtyard. For many years the House was occupied by the Registrar General of Births, Marriages and Deaths and his staff but they have now vacated the premises and the State Rooms have become the Courtauld Institute of Art.

At the end of Lancaster Place turn right into The Strand. Here can be seen…

(71) Parish Church of St Mary Le Strand.

Dating from 1717 the present church is considered to be one of the best examples of the work of James Gibbs, 1682 - 1754, the Scottish Roman Catholic architect. Built of solid Portland stone, to reduce the noise from the 18th century traffic that passed either side of this island church, many of the internal fittings, font, pulpit, altar rails, etc., have survived, together with the plaster work of the ceiling. On a clear sunny day the light shines through the Madonna Blue glass adding a kind of mystic atmosphere to the east end of the building. The church has a special affiliation with Charles I, king and martyr - in January each year a service of commemoration of his execution is held here. Recently too the church has been adopted by the Women's Royal Naval Service (WRENS) with all the kneelers in the nave being embroidered by present and past members of the Service.

Walk along The Strand until another "island church" is seen this is…

(72) Parish Church of St Clement Danes.

In the 9th century Danish seamen who had once come to London as marauders, and later as settlers, were allowed to build themselves a church - just outside the jurisdiction of the City of London. They chose as their Patron Saint, Clement the third Bishop of Rome in succession to Saint Peter, who had suffered martyrdom according to legend by being tied to an anchor of a ship and then cast overboard. His emblem, an anchor, can still be seen marking the boundaries of the parish today. At the time of the amalgamation of St Mary Le Strand and St Clement Danes Parishes in the 1950s, the latter's parish house was sold. Appropriately it was not called the Vicarage but the Anchorage! Today the church is the Mother Church of the Royal Air Force and in the spacious nave floor can be seen the crests of all the squadrons and units of the Air Force. On the pillars around the church are the badges of the various Air Force Commands. As in the previous church the kneelers here are the painstaking work of a dedicated body of embroiderers. During the Second World War the building was gutted but it has faithfully been restored by Sir Christopher Wren's original designs. In the crypt of the church is the baptistery with the modern font being the gift of the Royal Norwegian Air Force.

On leaving the church walk into the forecourt where there are three statues of interest. The Statue of Lord Dowding unveiled in October 1988 by Queen Elizabeth the Queen Mother, was the work of Faith Winter, paid for by public subscription and commemorates the man who master-minded the Battle of Britain during the Second World War. To the right of the door stands "Bomber Harris" chief of the R.A.F. Bomber Command during the second world war.

The other statue is of William Gladstone, 1809 - 1898, by Hamo Thornycroft, 1850 - 1925, and shows the former Prime Minister surrounded by four groups of bronze figures that represent Brotherhood, Aspiration, Education and Courage. Between the groups are shields depicting the arms of some of the counties and boroughs that he represented in Parliament.

Four times each day the bells of the church peal out "Oranges and Lemons" - a tune that has made the church world famous.

Across the roadway from the church stands the Royal Courts of Justice. At the meeting place of The Strand and Fleet Street formerly stood Temple Bar.

(73) Monument to Temple Bar.

While never a fortified entrance to the City of London, Temple Bar marked the limits of the jurisdiction of the Lord Mayors of London. It can best be equated with a frontier post between different countries - a place where people entering and leaving the country/city could be checked, tolls imposed, and undesirables turned away. Originally the Bar was little more than a chain across the roadway, but it was later developed into a gatehouse with rooms over. On the roof were displayed the heads of the men who had been beheaded for their crimes in and around the City. People would come and look at the heads - one man earnt his living by hiring out spy-glasses, at a 1/4d a time, for the curious to get a better, closer look at the heads. Other gates of the City were used in a similar way, and it is from this practice that the saying "counting heads" has evolved. It was the duty of the gate-house keeper to climb to the top of the gates every morning to make sure that ALL the heads were still there! It was not unknown for friends and relations of those executed to remove their heads after dark, while certain foreign merchants would pay heavily to buy the heads and turn them into drinking cups. The theory was that if poison were put in them they would splinter and so save the life of the drinker! When the King or Queen of England visits the City of London, the Lord Mayor meets them here and offers them the State Sword of the City. The Monarch touches the Sword and returns it to the Lord Mayor who then leads the King or Queen into the City. In 1878 the Bar was demolished and later rebuilt at Cheshunt in Hertfordshire where it was intended to be the grand entrance into the grounds of Theobalds House. Today, it is rotting away in its country retreat, although there have been plans over the last decade or more to restore it and bring it back to the City of London where it rightly belongs. In its place there is a monument designed by Sir Horace Jones the City Architect, with the dragon of the coat of arms of the City standing proudly on the top.

(74) Parish boundary mark.

Set into the pavement close to the wall of No.1 Fleet Street is the parish boundary mark of St Clement Danes (note the anchor). Adjacent to this is the mark for the next parish, St Dunstan in the West.

Passing through the invisible boundary which divided the two Cities of London and Westminster, enter into the City of London.

Almost immediately, on the right hand side there are two gated archways - the first roadway is Middle Temple Lane leading down to one part of The Temple. The next archway leads to the Temple Church and the Inner Temple. (A detailed visit to the Temple is included in Riverside Walk).

(75) Prince Henry's Room.

Over the archway entrance to Inner Temple Lane there is an early 17th century building known as the Prince Henry's Room. There are several stories recorded regarding the origins of the room, the most persistent being that it was built as the Council Room for the Duchy of Cornwall, and that the first floor room was set aside for the use for the Prince of Wales. This is borne out by the "fleur-de-lis" together with the motto "Ich Dien" (I Serve) both on the outside of the building, as well as in the plaster work of the room itself. Today the Room is under the control of the City Corporation with a Samuel Pepys Exhibition of "Pepysiana" on permanent loan from the Samuel Pepys Club. The Club was formed in 1903 with a membership at that time of 73, the age of Samuel Pepys when he died.

Walk down Fleet Street until Bride Lane is reached here can be found…

(76) Parish Church of St Bride's Fleet Street.

St Bridget was a 6th century Irish saint whose one great claim to fame was her ability to change water into beer! To appreciate the history and the development of the site of the church, it is advisable to visit the exhibition in the crypt. Here are displayed many of the items found in the excavations that took place after the bombing of the church in the last War, together with other "bits and pieces" that make up the local story. On the ground floor of the church the arrangements of the seating is collegiate, that is like a college chapel with the seating facing across the church instead of towards the east end. Wander around and find the beautiful terracotta work of Margery Meggit's Virginia Wade, the first child to be born in New Virginia of English parents. Close by is the font that was built for the Parish Church of St Helen's Bishopsgate, when that church was given a new one they disposed of their old one. Admire from the screen at the west end of the church the paintings on the wall of the east end - the apse, rounded end to the building, is an optical illusion.

After a while leave the church by the north west door and return to Fleet Street once more. On rejoining Fleet Street, turn right and walk along to Ludgate Circus and there turn right again. Walk down New Bridge Street towards Blackfriars Bridge **(21).** At the end of the street cross under the roadway by the subway and exit by the steps which lead to Blackfriars Stations. Walk along the pavement on the left hand side of the bridge, noting once again, the pillars that used to support the railway lines from the station across the river. On reaching the southern end of the bridge descend the stairs which lead to the pathway underneath the railway arches. Follow the path through until the…

(77) Founderers' Arms Public House.

*The public house which is part of a recent
development here takes its name from the
Worshipful Company of Founderers of the City
of London who were often expelled from the
City's confines by virtue of the noise and smell
that their trade invoked. Were they here at some
time of their history?*

From the public house there is a pleasant
riverside walk with a wide vista across the
river of the City. Along the south bank can
be seen...

(78) Bankside Power Station.

*Designed by Sir Giles Gilbert Scott, 1880 -
1960, the station became operational in 1963
but has stood idle since 1980. It will soon
become part of the Tate Gallery.*

(79) Wren's House.

*Sir Christopher Wren, 1632 - 1723, lodged here
at the time that he was supervising the
building of St Paul's Cathedral. Next to the
house are the lodgings of the Provost and
Canons of Southwark Cathedral.*

(80) Site of the new Globe Theatre.

*Here the late Sam Wannamaker has built a
replica of Shakespeare's Globe Theatre together
with a Shakespearean Study Centre.*

At the end of the riverside walk ascend the
stairs which lead to Southwark Bridge.
Cross the roadway. Turn left and walk over
the bridge. At the northern end turn right
into Upper Thames Street where, on the
opposite of the roadway is...

(81) St Michael Paternoster Royal
Church.

*This is "Dick Whittington's" church, who was
responsible in the 14th century for rebuilding
the early 12th century church that had fallen
into disrepair. In the Great Fire of 1666 the*

*church was destroyed and afterwards rebuilt by
Wren, it suffered severe damage in the Second
World War when a "flying-bomb", a V2, fell in
the vicinity. The present building owes its
careful restoration to Elidir Davies whose
painstaking care has so beautifully restored it to
its former glory. Today the church is 'home' to
the Mission to Seamen the Church of England's
missionary society with the responsibility for
working among seamen of all nations. Among
the original 17th century fittings that have
been replaced are the pulpit, ascribed to
Grinling Gibbons, 1648 - 1721, the reredos (the
carved woodwork behind the Holy Table) and
the lectern, all of which have been returned to
their original positions in the church. The great
brass 17th century candelabra come from the
nearby, demolished, Parish Church of All
Hallows the Great. All the glass in the
windows of the church are 'new' with the one
over the entrance doorway depicting Richard
Whittington with his cat.*

Continue to walk along Upper Thames
Street, passing under the Cannon Street
Station railway bridge, (with a possible
slight diversion down Cousins Lane to
look across the river towards the Anchor
public house on the opposite bank). On the
northern bank, the walk continues to
London Bridge - access is gained by way of
the stairs from the Lower Thames Street
side of the bridge. Walk across the bridge
on the left hand side of the roadway.
Pause, once again to admire the view
towards the Tower of London.

At the southern end, turn left down Tooley
Street, where on the left hand side is...

(82) St Olave's House.

*Built on the site of the 11th century church
dedicated in memory of St Olaf, or Olave, King
of Norway, who in 1014 helped King Ethelred
defend the City against the invading Danes.
The building was finally demolished in 1928
after having been destroyed more than once by
fire. There is an inscription on the building*

together with a mosaic of St Olave that tells the story of the church.

The walk along Tooley Street may not be the most inspiring in London with developments still being carried out in the middle portion of the street, but however, just past St Olave's House, is a development that should not be missed…

(83) Hays Galleria and adjacent buildings.

From the drab 19th century, sadly neglected warehouses the developers and their architects have produced a new "London Bridge City" with a charm all its own, with a selection of offices, shops, and even a hospital that will amaze visitors well into the next century. It is possible to eat, drink and to be merry all at the same time here! Those who want just to look and see what is there can also do this at their own leisure pace. A riverside walk, once again, opens up vistas across the river towards the City of London, with the Tower of London and Tower Bridge forming an important part of the skyline at this moment of time. Just to sit and look encourages one to forget the present and to look to the future. Well done the developers and their architects!

Return, however reluctantly, to Tooley Street, tempted perhaps to visit the London Dungeon on the opposite side of the roadway, with its gruesome stories of Medieval London - torture and all. Walk along Tooley Street, past the South London College, once the St Olave's Grammar School, to Tower Bridge Road. Here turn left and cross the river for the last time by way of the bridge.

(84) Tower Bridge.

There were many designs submitted for a new bridge that would separate the Upper and Lower Pools of London's Docks in the 19th century. These were a sliding bridge, which had double locks that enabled the river to continue its way while ships passed through the lock and a high level bridge that did not interfere with either the traffic on land or the ships on the river. Finally the committee that the City Corporation had set up to consider the matter voted in favour of the design of its own architect - Sir Horace Jones, 1819 - 1887, with J Barry Wolfe as the engineering expert to assist him. His ideas were slightly modified after his death, and the construction took place between 1886 and 1894 when the bridge was officially opened.

Since that time "these steel skeletons clothed in stone" have come to symbolise London, and have been adopted by the London Tourist Board as part of their official badge. The "blue-badged" guide-lecturer of the London Tourist Board proudly wears the bridge as part of their insignia. These are the guides who have qualified under the very stringent examinations of the London Tourist Board, and have earnt the privilege to wear the much sought after "blue-badge". Today the bridge offers panoramic views from its walkways, an exhibition, filmshow, museum and gift shop and has progressed from being the gateway into the Upper Pool of London into a rival tourist attraction to the nearby Tower of London. It is a sight not to be missed in your journey "Across the bridges of London".

From the bridge, it is a short walk along Tower Bridge Approach Road to Tower Hill and the underground station from which the walk started.

Notes

Keep up to date

If you would like a full list and to be kept
updated on all publications available from
Morning Mist, please send a postcard with
your name and address to:

Marketing
Morning Mist Publications
PO Box 108, Reigate
Surrey RH2 9YP.

T-Shirt only £6.95

A T-Shirt depicting the front cover of this
book is available from the publisher.

The T-Shirt is white and comes in one size only *(large)*.

Please send me.............T-Shirts. I enclose cheque/P.O. for

£..............made payable to Morning Mist Publications.

Please send your remittance to:

Marketing
Morning Mist Publications
PO Box 108, Reigate
Surrey RH2 9YP.